We Christians are hard to take seriously sometimes, because we often get so easily zealous about a "righteous" position that hinges on a chock-full-of-baloney premise.

But righteousness must be based on the razor-sharp truth of God's Word as our major premise, on honest and well-informed truth about a situation as our minor premise, and on truly Spirit-guided conclusions.

Fine Lines will show you how to tap your resources of true righteousness and how to be sure you are putting God's righteousness to work in your life.

FINE LINES

Knowing God's
Right/Wrongs
for Your Life

BILL STEARNS

Here's Life Publishers

Published by
HERE'S LIFE PUBLISHERS, INC.
P.O. Box 1576
San Bernardino, CA 92402

HLP Product Number 951434
Printed in the United States of America

Library of Congress Cataloging-in-Publication Data

Stearns, Bill.

Fine lines.

Bibliography: p.

1. Christian ethics.   I. Title.
BJ1251.S8145   1986   241   86-9838
ISBN 0-89840-128-3 (pbk.)

FOR MORE INFORMATION, WRITE:

L.I.F.E. — P.O. Box A399, Sydney South 2000, Australia
Campus Crusade for Christ of Canada — Box 300, Vancouver, B.C. V6C 2X3, Canada
Campus Crusade for Christ — Pearl Assurance House, 4 Temple Row, Birmingham B2 5HG, England
Lay Institute for Evangelism — P.O. Box 8786, Auckland 3, New Zealand
Great Commission Movement of Nigeria — P.O. Box 500, Jos, Plateau State Nigeria, West Africa
Campus Crusade for Christ International — Arrowhead Springs, San Bernardino, CA 92414, U.S.A.

This one is for
beloved Megan Hope

Contents

Foreword

Making moral decisions is more difficult today than ever. Not only are the pressures greater, but we also face issues that other generations did not encounter: abortion on demand, the ability to have a sex change operation, and a blizzard of moral choices ranging from divorce to videos. Each of these situations forces us into a moral choice.

In this book Bill Stearns helps us sift through our options by applying biblical principles to the cloudy moral decisions of life. If you are expecting him to tell you what to do, though, you will be disappointed. He's more interested in having you think through the process of decision-making than having you find the right answer by checking the table of contents.

Our generation is not willing to accept the moral opinions of others without personal conviction and thought. This book guides the traveler through the wilderness of secular theories of morality but eventually ends with an explanation of the enduring principles of Scripture. En route, there is plenty of opportunity for personal reflection and moral reasoning. There's no doubt but that the reader will be much better prepared for those agonizing moral decisions he will inevitably encounter as he walks along the path of life.

Here's a book for those who are beyond the "It's right because I said so!" kind of authoritarianism that has often caused cynicism within the church. The author gives a rationale for biblical principles, and shows that human reason left to itself will be self-defeating when confronting moral choices. I trust the book will have a wide circulation.

— Dr. Erwin W. Lutzer
Senior Pastor
The Moody Church, Chicago, IL

1
Righteousness Is Something You Do

Ethics: The discipline that deals with the goodness or evil of human choices.

The definition is simple. The choices often are not simple at all.

McKuen rubbed his eyes as the pediatric surgeon explained it again.

"Mr. McKuen, in layman's terms, the baby is extremely deformed, scarcely viable at this point. In all probability, it will live no more than a day."

"We'll need to think about it," said McKuen. "My wife. . ."

"Your wife is fine," the doctor said. "However. . ." He rose wearily. "However, the decision is yours. She's in no emotional condition to consider the options."

"God." McKuen was praying. He stood and glared at the surgeon. "Tell me again."

"Tell you what?"

"The options. What you need to do to keep it . . . to keep him alive."

The pediatrician repeated the exacting procedures, the pain the infant would undergo, the staggering costs involved. "And the entire undertaking will prolong the . . . the boy's life no longer than a month at most. If we're to go ahead, we'll need to begin immediately. If not, you and your wife can feel free to spend the rest of the day holding him." The doctor swung the door open as if it were lead. "We'll need your decision in, say, ten minutes. I'm sorry."

The door thudded shut, and McKuen collapsed back into the chair. He closed his eyes and finally identified the suffocating, nauseating feeling rising in him — he was terrified. "Three hours ago we were going to be a cute little family," he mumbled. "Now it's either let the baby die, or tell them to cut him and prod him for tens of thousands of dollars. And he. . ." He choked, "God, he's going to die anyway."

He kicked at the wastebasket, then slumped back to feel the fear boring like a drill near the nerves in his teeth.

Of course, not all situations are that dramatic. Sometimes the choices we must make come in a confusing mix of logic and nerve endings and pressure and desire. Like this one:

The midnight air off the lake was cool, the moon brilliant on the water. They had talked for several hours about this and that. Now she was sleepy — and a twinge of loneliness touched her.

"Why not come back to my cabin with me," he whispered, tracing his finger along her arm.

She stiffened. "I don't think so." Tossing a few more pebbles off the pier into the water, her eyes followed the smoke of the campfires, which hung like gauze beneath the incredible stars. "Hard to believe I've never seen a shooting star," she said absently.

"We are adults," he said. "And this might be a singles retreat, but. . ." Slowly he eyed her from head to toe.

"What do you think you're doing?" she demanded, incredulous that he'd fall to the old undress-her-with-his-eyes tactic.

"Perusing," he said.

"You peruse books," she snapped, "not people."

"You peruse works of art. And classics." He folded his arms and rested them against her knee. "You peruse poetry." In slow motion he stretched to kiss her cheek.

She turned away.

"It's a good night for snuggling." He stood. It was his last pitch, delivered in a perfect imitation of W.C. Fields. "Ah, yes, my dear. A good man is hard to find. And this, m'lady, could have been your lucky night."

She smiled and rolled her eyes.

He pointed up at the night sky, pantomiming a pistol, and crooked his thumb.

A star fell.

Coolly raising the pistol-finger to his lips, he puffed as if blowing away the smoke, and turned to saunter toward the cabins.

"Wait," she said.

Now I admit those two scenes don't present the usual ponderous dilemmas studied in classical ethics.

The blockbuster dilemmas are usually hypothetical. A popular one is: Suppose you're a World War II German citizen, hiding Jews. When the Nazi Gestapo asks, "Are you hiding any Jews?" do you answer, "I cannot tell a lie!"? Another one is: Suppose you're in a sinking lifeboat. You're a doctor so you'll be needed by survivors, and yet someone must be thrown out of the boat or all will perish. Whom do you throw overboard?

The classical dilemmas of ethics *are* approachable, but only by those people who have a solid system of personal ethics firmly in place. And it's here — in the quandaries of personal ethics — that our study together will develop our ethical skills. We'll primarily consider the more mundane questions of our non-hypothetical lives, such as: Is it right to enter a state lottery? Should I be involved in a dance group? Should I subscribe to a cable TV system which occasionally shows racy movies? Is it sinful to drive a few miles an hour over the speed limit? Can I step outside the back door when avoiding a phone caller and have my spouse say I'm "not in"? What is right and wrong in an unmarried couple's physical relationship? The Bible says, "Don't be drunk," but what about moderate drinking?

Many Christians feel that the study of ethics is way out of their league, even when dealing with the kitchen-table variety of questions about right and wrong. They can't imagine trying to face such thinkers as Nietzsche, Kierkegaard, Kant or Plato. But relax. We won't be bantering around philosophical curiosities with the great thinkers of history. We will be bantering around some of the ornery, ethical questions of our own life-styles. And you'll surprise yourself by the end of our study. You'll have formed the basis for a comprehensive, workable, personalized system of right and wrong — a system which will eventually allow you to tackle some of the great ethical questions that have confounded thinkers for centuries.

Responsibility

If you have entered a living relationship with Jesus Christ, you're supposed to know how to determine good and evil in your own life; to live ethically and morally — without compromise or hypocrisy — in the midst of a crooked, perverse, crazy and complex society; to be able, without contradiction, to pass your knowledge on to others, to the next generation.

But before the mandates get too scary, let me put them in more familiar terms: You've been given the responsibility to be righteous.

"With the heart man believes, resulting in righteousness" (Romans 10:10).

"What do I do?" the father asked me. "I mean, I know kids get into these things early nowadays, but. . . You're a Christian, right?" He uncrumpled the note again and smoothed it out in front of me. "I mean, look at the language! Here, look at this part: 'Did you like it when I did it to you on the watertower?' He's only a sophomore, Stearns. Maybe I'm over-reacting, huh? So what's the right thing to do now? Just give me a couple of ideas, okay?" He crumpled the note again and groaned. "Good grief. On the watertower. When I was his age. . ."

Apparently the father came to me because he understood that Christians, connected mystically to the righteous God of the universe, have something to do with morality, with ethics, with righteousness.

Christians are to "hunger and thirst for righteousness" (Matthew 5:6), to "pursue righteousness" (1 Timothy 6:11).

It's not that following the ways of righteousness allows us to glide past inconveniences like suffering and persecution (see Matthew 5:10; 1 Peter 3:14), and not that righteousness will bring us big rewards in this life. Ask a Christian businessman if it's easier to make a profit by being honest, or crooked. If he's honest, he'll have to say, "Better a little with righteousness than much gain with injustice" (Proverbs 16:8, The New International Version).

But even Christians have problems with being "good." In fact, sometimes we may wonder, "Why be good at all?"

In sixth grade, I'd purposely tell the teacher I didn't know an answer when I did; I'd knock over Ellen Nitler's stack of books; I'd smear enchiladas on the cafeteria tabletops. I didn't want to be pegged as a wimp who was always good. There was no advantage in goodness. After all, why do what's right, when what's wrong is so intriguing? Fortunately, when I became a man I put away childish things, and realized I'm to be righteous because God is righteous: "Everyone who does what is right is born of Him. . . . He who does what is right is righteous, just as He (God) is righteous" (1 John 2:29, 3:7, NIV).

It's obvious that, as God's children, we are to resemble our Father by knowing and doing what is right. But that's not always easy.

Think through — don't just read through — the following:
- Is it right or wrong for you to drink four cups of coffee daily? Why?
- Is it right for you to attend a movie that is rated "R" (restricted to those seventeen or older because of violence or profanity or nudity)? Why or why not?
- Is it right or wrong for you to keep $200 you happen to find on the street?
- Richard Wurmbrand was tortured by the communists for his faith in Christ. Much of the torture was designed to make him reveal the names of other believers. In *Stronger Than Prison Walls*, Wurmbrand

writes, "I lie to the Communist examining officers, and I must say I do it with delight." Wurmbrand relates his situation to that of Rahab (Joshua 2), who lied and was later commended (Hebrews 11:31). If you had been in Wurmbrand's or Rahab's position, would it have been right or wrong for you to lie? Why or why not?

Face it: Sometimes it's tough to know what is right even for us as individuals.

And it gets a little more complicated when you consider that our righteous responsibility doesn't end at our noses.

"Righteousness exalts a nation" (Proverbs 13:34).

We believers are to be the purifying "salt of the earth" and illuminating "light of the world" (see Matthew 5:13,14) in a rotting gloomy society.

The impact of 45 million evangelicals in the American society, for instance, has eye-opening potential. Rifkin and Howard, in *The Emerging Order: God in the Age of Scarcity,* see the Christian community in America as a significant alternative to the secular society. They point out that Christians have developed total church living complexes (with homes, stores, banks, and beauty shops), Christian motels, TV networks, over 1,300 radio stations, 2,300 Christian bookstores, million-dollar publishing and record companies, nationwide directories of Christian businesses and competent educational systems with over a million students in 5,000 schools. The influence of such a unified group has tremendous potential. But does that influence reflect true biblical righteousness, or simply conservative opinions and legalistic negativism?

In Christianized countries, religious righteousness has more often brought accusations of hypocrisy and misery than it has admiration for the peaceable fruits of real righteousness. As early as 1835, a common taunt in the U.S. and England was "Continence, mysticism and melancholia — three new infirmities introduced by Christ." Thirty years later, the poet Swinburne lamented, "Thou hast conquered, O pale Galilean; the world has grown grey with thy breath."

The true ethical and moral impact of Christendom in our culture depends on the ethical/moral standards maintained by individual Christians. How would your answers to the following impact your culture with "salt" and "light"?

- If your spouse is divorcing you and you've been separated for three months, is it okay to begin casual dating? Why or why not?
- If you meet an illegal alien who has escaped from a war-torn country, should you turn him in to the authorities who will deport him? Why or why not?
- Is it right or wrong to buy a condominium in what was once a welfare hotel, knowing that dozens of indigents were turned out into the streets so the condos could be developed? Why or why not?

"Lead the many to righteousness" (Daniel 12:3).

Christians are responsible to live in righteousness for the sake of their own integrity, for the curing and influence of society, and for the kids.

If you're immersed in the tough job of parenting right now, or if you ever plan to grow kids, you've got a job to do on the next generation, on the ten-year-olds who will come of age in the 21st Century, on the teenagers who are forming values in this tumultuous age of transformation which is much like what the magazine *Futurist* calls "the Reformation, the Industrial Revolution, and the Renaissance combined."[1]

The well-intentioned parents of the 1950s who trained their youngsters in the familiar conclusions of "acceptable" morality contributed one of the key factors to the wild and loose '60s counter-culture. Teenagers encountered unfamiliar dilemmas Mom and Dad had never dreamed of. So the 1964 kid had no rules covering the wild, new opportunities to slug acid-spiked Kool-Aid at rock concerts with sexually liberated peace children who cried "Death to the establishment." Not only did the 1964 kid have no ready-made rules that made sense, he further had no reasonable structure to formulate his own rights and wrongs. Consequently, an aura of diseased "free-love" and burned brains and jagged relationships still overshadows much of the good of that era.

The point is this: It will happen again. A generation that suddenly faces new ethical and moral dilemmas its parents never faced will desperately need a solid framework to develop its own applications of right and wrong. How can you equip kids to live in righteousness when they could face questions like:
• If my parent is being kept alive only by a resuscitator, is it okay for me to "pull the plug"? Why or why not?
• What does *God* say about the genetic restructuring of our test-tube fetus?
• Is our use of nuclear weapons right or wrong? Why?

If you feel a little resentful about having to answer the "why's" of your conclusions, take comfort — you're not alone. Many people today resist the idea that God or anybody else might ask them to give an account of what they believe and why. But especially if you plan to lead kids in righteousness, expect your ethics to be peppered with "why's."

It's an unfortunate era when parents' and authorities' decrees of rights and wrongs are countered constantly with, "Why?" But, as one campus minister to youth explained, "Today's young person is being *taught* to ask questions, to probe, to seek, to wonder why, and not to accept what seems true until it has been proven." But maybe it's not such an unfortunate situation after all — since it forces parents and authorities to give right/wrong conclusions, to evaluate how they arrived at those conclusions, and to ascertain the *value* they're trying to enforce. Molding rights and wrongs from solid values will stand us in good stead in the un-dreamed-of ethical dilemmas of the future. A strict application of behavior modification might ensure that our children act according to *our* conclusions of right and wrong, but a consistent teaching of values and the *how-tos* of biblical ethics are the keys to leading them in real righteousness.

Righteousness

So we've got our righteous responsibilities — to ourselves, to our society, to our children. And since the responsibility seems so critical, maybe we should quickly investigate this term we've been throwing around so nobly. Just what is *righteousness?*

In the Old Testament, six Hebrew words are translated *righteous.* In every case, the focus is on a single idea: The righteous person is right with God. In the New Testament, the Greek word for *righteous* is often rendered *just* (see Matthew 1:19; Mark 6:20; Luke 1:17; John 5:30), which also implies being right with God. In fact, in the Greek New Testament, the words for *justification* and *righteousness* come from exactly the same root. The just person *(dikaos)* who observes his fulfillment of duty *(dike)* in right acts *(dikaioma)* develops a character of righteousness *(dikaiosman).* We're familiar with the idea that Abraham was "justified by faith," but somehow we're not so sure about the additional thought that his "faith was reckoned for [literally, ' with a view to'] righteousness" (Romans 4:3,5,9,22). A person who is justified — who is right with God — is righteous!

Most Christians would pass a pop quiz on the question, Are you justified as a Christian? They would respond, "Of course, I've been justified as a gift by His grace through the redemption which is in Christ" (Romans 3:24). But unfortunately many might flunk on the question, Are you *righteous* as a Christian? even though having been declared *just* is synonymous with having been declared *righteous.*

The point is this: Contrary to the knock-down-drag-outs of the typical church business meeting, Christians are righteous. You as a believer can nod to yourself in the mirror and say,"I am righteous," because God has actually given you His righteousness:

- "The righteousness of God has been manifested . . . through faith in Jesus Christ for all those who believe" (Romans 3:21,22).
- "By his [God's] doing you are in Christ Jesus, who became to us wisdom from God, and righteousness" (1 Corinthians 1:30).
- "He made him who knew no sin to be sin on our behalf, that we might become the righteousness of God in Him" (2 Corinthians 5:21).
- The apostle Paul counted all things rubbish, "that I may gain Christ and may be found in Him, not having a righteousness of my own derived from the law, but that which is through faith in Christ, the righteousness which comes from God on the basis of faith" (Philippians 3:8,9).

Now, if you're like me, you're telling yourself, "Don't get excited about being righteous. I mean *really* righteous. All these verses just point out the vague abstraction you've always known: You are spiritually pie-in-the-sky in God's sight, righteous in your *standing* — in your *position* as a Christian. You're *declared* righteous, but you're really not. That positional kind of righteousness isn't real in an earthly way; it won't help much in your responsibility to *live* righteously. Your actual state is anything but righteous.

What about it? Is righteousness unreal? Or is it practical and available to us in our nitty-gritty, planet-Earth life?

I believe that our righteousness as believers is not floating vaguely in the heavens. We actually have been *given* God's righteousness here and now. We are new creations when we receive Christ (2 Corinthians 5:17) because God gives us new natures. We are "partakers of the divine nature" (2 Peter 1:4).

This new nature is a "new self, which in the likeness of God has been created in righteousness and holiness of the truth" (Ephesians 4:24). So righteousness actually exists as a quality in the new nature of a believer because God by His righteous Spirit exists within him (Romans 8:9).

The challenge of the Christian's life is to show on the outside what we have on the inside — an infinite reservoir of potential righteousness. And, naturally, that's just the process performed by the Holy Spirit in us believers — transforming our outward lifestyle to match our inner, new nature. Our Spirit-powered metamorphosis, termed *sanctification,* allows righteous attitudes and acts: It's "by the sanctifying work of the Spirit that you may obey Jesus Christ" (1 Peter 1:2). A believer who walks in the Spirit can resist unrighteousness with a vengeance: "Walk by the Spirit, and you *most definitely* will not fulfill the desire of the old sin nature" (translation of the emphatic, double negative of Galatians 5:16). Righteousness isn't just something we *can* have; it's something we *have* and can *do* in nitty-gritty, everyday life.

So on the authority of God's Word, you can tell yourself: "As a believer, I have the righteousness of God in me." Regardless of your failures, regardless of your feelings of unworthiness — God's Word states that you've got everything you need to fulfill your responsibilities in right living, in righteousness.

Even for those of us who struggle with choices between right and wrong — and who doesn't, at one time or another? — we do want righteousness, don't we? Even when you're ready to toss it all in and live like everyone else, there's always that still, small voice insisting you could *be* somebody for God; you could live in the wisdom that transcends the humdrum compromising the quiet desperation of the masses. You could make a difference. You can join other believers as "we through the Spirit by faith are waiting [better translated, 'looking with intense yearning'] for the hope of righteousness [better, 'the hoped-for righteousness']" (Galatians 5:5). We want to be righteous people — not wimpy do-gooders or holier-than-thou nitpickers, but righteous as God is righteous. So the big question is how to tap our resources of righteousness — how to be "filled with the fruit of righteousness which comes through Jesus Christ" (Philippians 1:11).

And that's what this book is all about — how to put God's righteousness to work in the practicalities of right living. You can expect that we won't spend much time discussing human efforts at righteousness, which were spiritual-life killers among the brethren of the apostle Paul: "For I bear them witness that they have a zeal for God, but not in accordance with knowledge. For not knowing about God's righteousness, and seeking to establish their own, they did not subject themselves to the righteousness of God" (Romans 10:2,3). Little in the world reeks as much as human self-righteousness (see Isaiah 64:6).

On the other hand, you can expect that we will spend time discussing at least three major topics:
• God's Word; for it is the "word of righteousness" (Hebrews 5:13).

- Faith; for the righteous "shall live by faith" (Romans 1:17).
- The role of the Holy Spirit in our lives; since "the righteousness of the law" is fulfilled in us — not *by* us — "who walk . . . after the Spirit" (Romans 8:4, KJV).

So move over, Nietzsche. We're about to examine the history, the foundation stones and the practical applications of God's system for determining right and wrong.

2
Hodge-Podge Ethics

Not long ago, a Christian friend told me he was so confused about a situation he was ready to flip a coin to see what he should do. The dilemmas we find ourselves in sometimes get crazy. I've seen my share.

Once, I worked for a drilling company on an off-shore oil rig in the Gulf of Mexico. My crew would often be evacuated to on-shore motels when a hurricane threatened. One night, as a hurricane swirled around New Orleans, we finished supper in a restaurant, and Maurice, the crew derrickman, ordered an after-dinner drink. In roughneck style, he accosted the waitress with the idea that he could order drinks from the bar and she could charge them to the company on his food bill.

She refused.

"Do it!" he shouted.

"No, that's unethical," she stated firmly.

Maurice leaped into an oilfield-style tirade. "It is okay!"

"It's not!" I munched my French fries and stared in amazement at this clash of ethical systems. One system gauged fudging on company expense accounts as permissible, and the other judged it as flat-out wrong.

Three women lay on the sand. The one with the yellow plastic sunguards on her eyes said, "I brought my chicken. Pastor said we'd be eating right after the games for the children."

"That's if we can get them out of the lake," said the oldest one. She shaded her eyes and frowned at the water. "Elma, look at that."

Elma plucked off the sunguards, twitched her head up and said, "That's the Douglas girl. Looks like it's painted on."

The youngest woman sat up. "Oh, Mother, that's just because it's wet. When the fabric gets wet, it just clings more. . ."

Elma still craned to look. "Disgusting. Just because she's developing doesn't mean she's got to flaunt it at the church picnic. Look at that — look at that!"

"At least it's one piece," said the grandmother.

"Yeah, Mom," said the youngest. "Remember our fights about my two-piece bathing suits? And look at you now!"

Elma pulled a towel across her bare midriff. "This is a lot more modest than those two-piece things you were trying to wear. Besides. . ." She replaced her sunguards. "Besides. . ."

The Douglas girl walked by and smiled.

"Shall we tell her?"

"Tell her what?"

"Why, that her suit is immodest."

"Immodest to whom?" said the young woman. "To your generation, Grandma? To Mom's? To mine? Or to hers? Who's to say exactly?"

The older woman said nothing. Then Elma said, "I wonder."

"Wonder what?"

"I wonder if I brought enough chicken."

It happens all the time. One person thinks driving two miles over the speed limit is a cardinal sin; another laughs it off as a totally amoral issue. One generation says that two-piece bathing suits are immoral; the next generation claims that sin is only in the eye of the beholder.

C.S. Lewis, in a series of radio talks on right and wrong, compared ethics to a convoy of ships. He said that in order to keep the ships from colliding and damaging each other, certain rules must be observed. In order to maintain those convoy rules, each individual ship must observe certain on-board regulations to keep the vessel seaworthy and operating properly. But a convoy will still destroy itself if there is rampant confusion about the convoy's destination. In the same way, strict moral regulations observed by each individual and between individuals in society can still result in chaos if there is no agreement on the ultimate values behind moral rules.

Lewis concluded that the dizzying confusion of today's value systems demands more than just mindless good intentions: "Because Christ said we could get into His world only by being like children, many Christians have the idea that, provided you are 'good,' it doesn't matter being a fool."[1]

Measuring Sticks

Every person has his own mental measuring stick of what is acceptable, what's bad, what's good. These ethical scales can change as notches are added or rearranged according to what is important to the person, what is valuable.

For example, measuring sticks notched with values of pleasure are hot-selling items these days. This ethical system yardstick is inscribed at the top with the old '60s slogan "If it feels good, do it!" The user contemplates an activity, an attitude, an incident. He then matches it against the measurement of how much pleasure it will bring, and concludes the activity is right if it feels good enough. Year after year, pop songs turn up with the crooning lyric, "It can't be wrong if it feels so right."

Andrea was a Sunday school kid. She knew all the traditional ethical conclusions. But there didn't seem to be any sense behind many of the old do's and don'ts. And changing herself to apparently unfounded, legalistic rules of conduct ("I don't see any commandment against casual cocaine in the Bible, and there's nothing about marriage ceremonies") wasn't being real and honest the way she felt God wanted Christians to be.

She felt wonderful on grass and easily moved to harder hallucinogens. "Why not?" she reasoned. "You use aspirin and drink coffee, don't you?" As time went on she lived more and more by her feelings. She loved deeply, and so she lived with guy after guy, but relationship after relationship fizzled quickly.

I talked with Andrea for hours one California afternoon. She was slow to analyze things — her thinking was dulled by dope — as we kicked around the problems of living by feelings, of determining rights and wrongs by what gives the most immediate pleasure.

I called her recently, and asked what living by feelings was like now, years later.

"I guess I was one of those whose 'god is their belly,'" she laughed. "I've found that, like David, God can still bless me and use me. I have a husband and kids, and am involved in new projects like going back to school and ministering at church. But it sure wasn't worth the trip!"

A second measuring stick is the one notched with values of prestige. In fact, people value prestige so much that they'll often do something to be admired even if it's painful: starve the kids in order to afford a classy car; mash feet into too-small shoes for a fashionable, petite look; repress painful emotions just to appear brave or respectable. Who hasn't sacrificed himself at one time or another to save his reputation?

Why has prestige become so important? The glee over disposable products in our society has caught naturalistic thinkers in an elaborate Chinese finger trap. The more people insist that we are only accidental products of an impersonal universe, the more the foreboding disposal expert, Death, forces them to conclude that man is simply a disposable product with the value of a taco carton — or, at best, a recyclable beer can. But when Joe Modern is told he's disposable, that he's nothing more than a certain configuration of atomic particles, it goes against his grain. He craves to be important, to be significant and valuable. The more he feels like a cosmic zero, the more he strives to *be* somebody, to make a mark on the universe, to win recognition and status.

For instance, once when I moved to an economically depressed area of the country, I was amazed to see that everyone who could afford a car at all drove huge, luxurious gas-hog models. It was as if they were compelled to tell the world, "See? I ain't poor!"

The philosopher Kierkegaard saw this frustration as the plague of modern man: People feel the alienation, the abysmal gap between who they think they are and who they *want* to be.

So the incredibly popular prestige scale of ethical values says, "If it'll make you look good, go for it." There are, of course, options available on the standard model. The stick may be inscribed with, "If everybody's doing it or has it, it's okay." (An old-timer I know calls this the Maggot Principle: A rotting possum carcass must be good stuff, since two million maggots can't be wrong!)

Regardless of the variations, a prestige measurement of right and wrong is basically a valuation of peer pressure. Although we usually relegate the peer pressure phenomenon to teenagers, it's alive and very well in young adult, middle age and elderly groups. People start smoking cigarettes, dive into debt, murder relationships and deny Christ because of peer pressure prestige. Don't look so sanctimonious: If you suddenly were sentenced to a solitary life on a desert island, how many peer-pressured activities and possessions would drop out of your life with no feeling of loss at all? Even old habits may be motivated solely by the desire to look good.

In fact, measuring sticks are a dime a dozen these days. Call it evolution: Here in the West, from a basic set of Judeo-Christian values, mutations by the dozens have developed. One ethical measuring stick is called "convenience" — so the abortion of an "inconvenient" fetus is right, according to the scale. Another stick places "democratic patriotism" as the most important value — so anything that's done to discourage communism is right, anything left-leaning is wrong.

Chuck Colson, in *Born Again,* discussed how his pre-Christian, Watergate crimes were perfectly right according to the value-scale of "loyalty": "Even if Nixon were lying, did it all matter really that much? Not really. Nixon was the President and it had always been my duty to defend him. That's what being a White House aide is all about — loyalty is the one imperative. . . . Misleading millions of Americans never crossed my mind."[2]

The break from a central Judeo-Christian value system leads naturally into a Pandora's Box of ideas about right and wrong. This mishmash actually is traceable in a society.

In the United States, for instance, the splintering of American value systems was obvious as early as the 1850s. In 1850, Nathaniel Hawthorne's striking novel of sin and guilt, *The Scarlet Letter,* pointed to a time when adultery in America would be tolerated, "as long as the two people sincerely love each other. . ." In contrast, Herman Melville's 1851 novel, *Moby Dick,* pointed back to a disappearing standard that recognized in the world a pattern of good and evil, of black-and-white morality. In 1854 Thoreau published *Walden,* which encouraged readers to march to the different drummer of individualism. Walt Whitman's 1855 *Leaves of Grass* advised, "Whatever satisfies the soul is truth." Ralph Waldo Emerson published several essays in 1856, teaching that Jesus Christ was only a spectacular man and that true morality is discovered only in man's natural, moral nature. And in 1859, Darwin's *Origin of the Species* was printed in England — and its immediate effect on American thinking is a good lesson on what an idea can do. So the 1850s was a wild decade, a sort of watershed in American history when the inevitability of a coming plethora of ethical value scales was obvious.

Nowadays, twelve people, citing twelve different right/wrong measuring sticks can argue that an issue is right, wrong, divine, demonic, entertaining, disgusting, irrelevant, critical, beautiful, obscene, before-its-time, or outdated. It's a period like the time of the book of Judges when everybody simply does what is "right in his own eyes" (Judges 21:25). It's the existential, democratic way: Everyone can be his own god.

Of course, the profusion of value system measuring sticks is only natural since "the lust of the flesh" (pleasure), "the lust of the eyes" (prestige), and "the boastful pride of life" (be your own god) are only natural expressions of the body, soul and spirit (1 John 2:16).

One problem in pick-a-card-any-card values comes when we realize how many choices there are. It's inevitable that, as a society, we're shaky on how to act around each other. As decent humans, we're anxious about doing what's best — but it's rough to figure out what's best when all values are relative, when rights and wrongs are just a matter of your preference. What's best on one well-accepted measuring stick can be worst on another: Advising your teenage daughter on birth control methods is brilliant and right according to one standard, but anathema according to another.

When was the last time you were in a sticky situation where you weren't quite sure if you were correct or not? I felt that uneasiness when I was in an auto accident, and it took the police three days to determine fault. I'd turned in front of an approaching car. (So I was wrong — right?) But the car had been speeding and wouldn't have hit me otherwise. (So I was right — right?) But a passenger in the other car was a pregnant lady, who was slightly injured. (I felt terribly guilty.) Needless to say, I didn't sleep well while waiting for the verdict. (I was found to be not at fault.)

Feeling unsure if you're right or wrong is unnerving, because we all have an innate awareness that wrong actions and attitudes invite negative results. The apostle Paul notes that even "men who suppress the truth in unrighteousness" have a foreboding sense that the universe punishes wrong, "for the wrath of God is revealed from heaven against all ungodliness and un-righteousness" (Romans 1:18, KJV). If you've ever helped in a childrens' shelter, you know you can pick out the abused children right away. The battered kids do something, then glance nervously at the attending adults to see if their action will bring punishment or not. Not knowing what to expect, trained under incon-sistent standards of what's acceptable and what isn't, even very young abused toddlers flinch at an adult's touch.

And that's a perfect metaphor for where we, as a culture, are ethically. As we try to pluralistically respect so many diverse standards, we're at odds with our tradition, with each other, and often with ourselves. We're not sure whether to expect blessing or judgment. Our staccato lives move so quickly that we seem to see right and wrong as irreconcilably blurred. If our society continues to be one in which individuals live by ethical systems that, in reality, are no ethical systems at all, our vision of right and wrong is destined to carry us to moral blindness.

Where does this hodge-podge of ethical measuring sticks come from?

Most are acquired. in the process of growing up. When my father lined up seven of us kids at the waste basket and demanded to know who threw the family Bible away, the principle was engraved on my gray matter: It is not right to throw Bibles in trash cans. All through life, values are assembled from a menagerie of experiences: It is wrong to stick a baby's finger into an electrical outlet; it is right to tell Grandma that you love her; it is right to do your own work on tests; it is wrong to forget to signal a turn. Values often come from simple, traditional sayings, such as, "Better dead than Red," or "Every boy has to sow a few wild oats."

Sometimes we adopt whatever ideas about right or wrong happen to be floating around us. Sometimes we swing to the opposite side in reaction. ("My parents spanked me as a kid, but I'll never spank my children.")

Regardless of where we acquired them, all the confusing variations of values boil down to three "canons" of ethical systems: antinomianism, situationalism and absolutism. In order to cut our way through the jungle undergrowth of widely-varying values that are choking us today, we Christians need to understand what these systems are and how they operate. Let's examine them.

3

Three Great Ethical Ideas that Don't Work

Mark Twain once remarked, "To be good is noble, but to show others how to be good is nobler — and not so much trouble." That's debatable. Through the centuries, one ethical genius after another has attempted to teach mankind a basis for values. And judging from the number of geniuses and the wild variety of their ethical tricks, the teaching of ethical philosophies has been quite a bit of trouble!

Antinomianism and Liberty

Antinomianism means "against law." As a philosophy, it preaches liberty and freedom from restrictions. It hums the naturalist, Protagorean anthem: "Man is the measure of all things." The only rules you must recognize are the rules you want to use. God doesn't exist, or He has died; either way you don't need to acknowledge any restrictions that supposedly have come from Him. The philosophy is as old as the question, "Indeed, has God said you shall not. . .?"

(Genesis 3:1), though it has lately found enthusiastic support in the existential movement. Existentialism suggests that man is his own isolated god in an indifferent universe, and he is startlingly free to choose what he will do with his inexplicable existence.

Friedrich Nietzsche, the German philosopher and poet, who called himself the "first immoralist," was an astute crusader for antinomian ethics. He taught that right and wrong, good and evil were not either/or: Right is not the opposite of wrong. Rather, Nietzsche held, right and wrong are merely general ideas on a continuum. Each individual is free to decide, according to his chosen set of values, what is better or worse. So an action can be right because it's "more right" than the worst action you can imagine.

Jean Paul Sartre, the French author-philosopher who died in 1980, carried the philosophy of freedom to its extreme in novels such as *Nausea.* It's not fun reading. Dostoyevsky, a 19th century Russian writer who had a Christian perspective, had challenged the antinomians with their horrifying problem: "If God is dead, then *all* is permitted."

Sartre seemed to respond, "Exactly."

Consequently, his fictional characters live in an uneasy universe which is so free of any guidelines that they are forced to conclude life is meaningless, frightening and completely absurd.

Situationalism and Love

Cratylus wrote, "Everything is in a state of transition and there is nothing abiding." This idea, that there are no changeless truths, sets the stage for the ethical philosophy of situationalism. Situationalism contends that everything changes, every experience is unique, and rights and wrongs can be discerned only according to love, the one universal standard.

Modern fans of situationalism assert that this philosophy at least recognizes limits to actions. There *are* rights and wrongs. And further, situationalism can even sound biblical, since the greatest commandment is to "Love the Lord your God. . . . And love your neighbor as yourself" (Matthew 22:36-40).

In 1928, Eberhard Grisebach of Germany suggested *Situationsethik* as the answer to man's moral questions. The basic idea is that a person will be right if motivated by love. During World War II, Dietrich Bonhoeffer, a Lutheran pastor, furthered the situation ethics picture by publishing a treatise on why it must be right to assassinate a man like Adolph Hitler. "The question of good," suggested Bonhoeffer, "is posed and is decided in the midst of each definite, yet unconcluded, unique and transient situation of our lives."

With this approach, a person doesn't need to figure out any systematic ethical structure, since each situation is intrinsically unique. Even the precepts observed and actions pictured in the life of Jesus were simply illustrations of how love acted in His day.

Bishop John A.T. Robinson and Joseph Fletcher in recent years have championed situation ethics by bringing up some of the notorious, sticky situations of right and wrong.

For instance, Fletcher tells the true story of a German infantryman named Bergmeier who was captured during the Battle of the Bulge and sent to a prisoner of war camp in Wales. Shortly thereafter, his wife, while searching for food for their three children, was picked up by a Soviet patrol and eventually sent to a prison camp in the Ukraine. After a few months, Bergmeier was released, and he returned to Berlin to find his family. He found his three children. Later, Mrs. Bergmeier learned that her family was desperately trying to find her. Release from the prison camp was allowed only in case of an illness requiring treatment the camp could not provide. Mrs. Bergmeier wrestled with the alternatives, and finally asked a sympathetic prison guard to impregnate her. When her condition was verified, she was returned to Germany because she had become a "liability" to the Russians. She reunited with her family, and they all welcomed the arrival of little Dietrich, who had brought their family together as no one else could.

Now since this self-sacrificing act of adultery was motivated by the woman's love for her family, wasn't her action right? Apparently, as long as her motivation was love, Mrs. Bergmeier could have gone further — stealing, lying, perhaps murdering. How far can a loving person's actions go before they become wrong? With situation ethics, who's to say?

The problems are obvious. Even Fletcher is vague as to what this all-encompassing love is, saying that the content of love varies from one situation to another. He says the love principle is impossible to pin down; it "rules us and yet does so without content." In other words, situation ethics requires that we make up the best version of what love is, and that we do it on the spot, as a right/wrong situation hits us. So much of the time, Fletcher admits, we are only making educated guesses.

Absolutism And Law

Now we come to some philosophical territory that is probably closer to home: the ethical arena of law. Absolutism — the belief that there are unchangeable rules of right and wrong — is often viewed as the religious school of ethics. Now, God's values, principles and commands *are* absolute (see chapter 4), but the philosophical absolutism we're now discussing usually contends that our applications of these rules are also absolute. It's perhaps closer to the biblical idea of ethics than are antinomianism and situationalism; and for that reason it's the most common counterfeit of biblical ethics.

Absolutism, as a philosophy, found its earliest proponent in Plato, who maintained that you will always be right if you stick to absolute rules of conduct. More recently, Emmanuel Kant suggested that it would be right to tell a maniac murderer where his potential victim was hiding, because it is wrong to lie.

The problems of absolutism are sometimes disturbing to Bible-believing Christians, since they equate this philosophy with the Bible's structure of determining right and wrong. Charles Spurgeon, the English preacher of the last century, once upset his listeners by preaching a stirring sermon on the fact that the New Testament approves the actions of Rahab the harlot — actions which involved her lying about her knowledge of Israelite spies (see Joshua 11:31; James 2:25). Many readers of the Old Testament squirm at the conflict of the law, "You shall not murder" (Exodus 20:13), with the Israelites' ordered killing of men, women and children (1 Samuel 15:1-3). God commanded that adulterers be stoned to death (Leviticus 20:10), and yet Jesus set free the woman taken in adultery, saying, "Go your way. From now on, sin no more" (John 8:3-11). The Bible commands that Christians obey even evil governing authorities, and yet Peter and John showed blatant, civil disobedience (Acts 4:1-20). Many believe suicide to be a cardinal sin; but since this is only gained by inference from the Bible, what do we say about the soldier who dives on a grenade to save a buddy? Since God commanded that the Sabbath — Saturday — be kept as His holy day, were the disciples wrong to start worshiping on Sunday, the first day of the week? Many scholars of absolutism, of course, contend that these conflicts are apparent only because of limited human thinking.

But whether these laws do or do not conflict (see chapter 4), absolutism is plagued with the reality that it's just not practical. That is, there seem to be so many "gray" areas that traditional rules and even biblical laws don't cover. And an even larger problem is that, when a person tries to observe all the rules, inevitably, callous legalism creeps in.

Supernatural Ethics

All human measuring sticks stem from one or more of these philosophical bases: liberty, love, or law. But there's the rub: Christians can't waste time and energy on natural, human ethics. Human systems are necessarily limited to human understanding. So even our brightest and best blunder.

It's all too easy, in our natural world, to fall unthinkingly into one of the human philosophies of right and wrong, or to react against one while backing into another. The man who was raised in an absolutist atmosphere will often swing pendulum-like toward a lawless lifestyle as an adult. On the other hand, the person trained with a certain set of standards may hang onto those rules because they are familiar and comfortable, not because they are right. Many people never evaluate their own values. Perhaps they are lazy, or perhaps they are afraid of being led beyond their depth.

But as C.S. Lewis emphasizes in *Mere Christianity,* a true understanding of right and wrong is a key to the meaning of the universe. So slow down for a few minutes and evaluate your own set of values.

Acknowledging the significance of human values is important. But catching the *synthesis* of law, love and liberty in biblical ethics is much more important. And how do we find that right measuring stick of truth?

> Thy word is truth (John 17:17, KJV).

How do we learn to *tap into* this truth?

> Solid food is for the mature, who by constant use have trained themselves to distinguish good from evil (Hebrews 5:14, NIV).

And,

> All Scripture is God-breathed and is useful for teaching, rebuking, correcting and training in righteousness, so that the man of God may be thoroughly equipped for every good work (2 Timothy 3:16,17, NIV).

So enough of humanity's incomplete and ultimately empty philosophies. Let's get into the Word of God, and learn what He has to say about living by the law and by love and in liberty.

For Study, Thought and Discussion

What and who were the greatest influences on your values?

Which of the three general processes — law, love or liberty — most closely describes your philosophy of determining right and wrong?

Have you reacted against values you were raised with? Have you ever examined them carefully?

List the people, things, experiences, feelings and goals that are most valuable to you.

4
Law: Going by the Book

God has the final say on right and wrong. His Word is absolute and authoritative — even when commands conflict.

Are there absolutes? Plato said yes. His list of basic eternal virtues — courage, temperance, wisdom and justice — were key elements in his utopian Republic. Protagorus, however, argued that since "Man is the measure of all things" and since man is a variable, life in the universe is intrinsically relative. Kant agreed with Plato; he urged that not only were there absolutes which were universal and unchangeable, but also that a person sticking to these absolute laws would always be right — even if he were to tell a murderer where his victim was to observe the absolute law against lying.

What Place Law?

A norm, from the Latin *norma,* is a rule, like a carpenter's square. It's a rule to mark and measure conduct as right or wrong. The norms of God's Word are eternally "good" and "holy" (Romans 7:12). The apostle Paul reminded Timothy, "We know that the law is good, if one uses it lawfully" (1 Timothy 1:8).

Unlawful use of the Book of God's norms has always been rampant: Jesus reprimanded the Sadducees, "You are mistaken, not understanding the Scriptures" (Matthew 22:29); the apostle Peter warned that some things in the Pauline epistles were "hard to understand, which the untaught and unstable distort, as they do also the rest of the Scriptures, to their own destruction" (2 Peter 3:16).

"Unlawful" ideas about law notwithstanding, God's norms as revealed in His Word are absolute. That is, they're eternally true (see Psalm 119:89; Isaiah 40:8; Matthew 24:35; Romans 3:31; 8:2; Galatians 6:2,13; James 1:25). Violating God's law is always wrong.

Jesus' testimony to the law is clear:

> "Do not think that I came to abolish the Law or the Prophets; I did not come to abolish, but to fulfill. For truly I say to you, until heaven and earth pass away, not the smallest letter or stroke shall pass away from the Law until all is accomplished. Whoever then annuls one of the least of these commandments, and so teaches others, shall be called least in the kingdom of heaven" (Matthew 5:17-19).

I think we can agree: God's norms are to be obeyed — "By this we know that we have come to know Him, if we keep His commandments" (1 John 2:3); "Whatever we ask we receive from Him, because we keep His commandments and do the things that are pleasing in His sight" (1 John 3:22); "By this we know that we love the children of God, when we love God and observe His commandments. For this is the love of God, that we keep His commandments; and His commandments are not burdensome" (1 John 5:2,3).

Just talking about commandments, rules and laws seems burdensome, doesn't it? But remember that many of us are still on the pendulum-swing reaction to Puritanical legalism. Also, the anti-establishment hoopla of the late 60s and early 70s brought insulting connotations to terms like "authority," "absolutes," "rules" and "law." So when it comes to discussing God's rules, quite a few of us Christians find we've adopted mindsets of mild lawlessness or relational ethics. But the ancient laws of God are alive and well, and they prescribe righteous living. Let's make sure we agree on what we mean by God's laws, then we'll tackle the hot spots of this foundation stone of ethics.

God's explicit and implicit laws are absolute. The Bible sometimes teaches these truths in the form of value-statements — such as, man is infinitely valuable because he was created in God's image (Genesis 1:26-27). These values are then reflected in broader principles that can be applied in various situations. It's critical to notice that the principles of Scripture are always reflective of God's value-statements. For instance, human value is mentioned in James 3:9: "With (the tongue) we bless our Lord and Father; and with it we curse men, who have been made in the likeness of God." The next verse moves from this value to put forth a principle: "From the same mouth come blessing and cursing. My brethren, these things ought not to be this way" (James 3:10).

The implicit guidelines that derive from God's value-statements are sometimes distilled into explicit *commandments,* such as "You shall not murder" (Exodus 20:13). The ethicist Oliver Barclay says that "the rules are fixed points which give teeth to the principles."[1] That is, the explicit rules of the Book are divine, absolute applications of the values and principles of God. "You shall not bear false witness against your neighbor"

(Exodus 20:16) and "Do not lie to one another" (Colossians 3:9) are Thus-saith-the-Lord, specific applications of biblical principles concerning how we treat each other.

For clarity in this discussion, let's keep in mind this hierarchy:

value

principle

command

Now, while God's commands — or norms — are absolute, our specific applications of His values and principles are not. For example, a basic New Testament principle is, "Your body is a temple of the Holy Spirit . . . therefore glorify God in your body" (1 Corinthians 6:19-20). When Ichabod Housermountain, a believer with severe gastric ulcers, applies this principle to eating an anchovy-peanut-butter pizza, he'll find that he would violate the principle if he were to eat. I, on the other hand, am ulcer-free and, applying the same principle, could eat with joy. Keep it clear for future reference: Our *personal applications* of God's true, eternal, absolute norms are not necessarily eternal absolutes.

Obviously the specific commands of the Bible don't cover every picky situation we will encounter in life. Thus, the values and principles stated in Scripture are the keys to discovering right and wrong in all the fuzzy areas not addressed by commands.

In Plato's *Euthyphoro,* the philosopher is asked whether the gods command these things because they are right, or whether these things are right because the gods command them. Knowing the loving God who is revealed to us in Scripture and by the Holy Spirit, we can believe that God's personal values are the reasons behind His norms — that He isn't arbitrarily making up rules to watch us squirm or rules for rules' sake. The norms and their corresponding values are reflections of His nature, of what's true in His universe, of how He lives life — and would live life if He were a human. His norms are the ultimate guidelines for living the best possible human life. For now, let's leave the rationale behind God's commandment-giving at the level of the Westminster Shorter Catechism: "Because God is the Lord and our God and Redeemer, we are bound to keep all His commandments." Absolute norms are absolute norms because they describe His absolute character. Because He's God, He gets to set the norms; or, more accurately, the norms are set. So it would certainly make sense for Him to tell us about them.

The Authority Of The Word Of God

Yannis Ritsos' "The Meaning of Simplicity" (translated by Edmund Keeley) suggests the power of true words:

Every word is a doorway

to a meeting, one often cancelled,

and that's when a word is true;

when it insists on the meeting.[2]

The truths of God's Word are insistent. Understanding the guidelines for the best possible life requires a solid understanding of the Word; I need to understand God's values, to know His principles and commands. But can I trust the Bible as the authoritative Word of God? So many people stumble over that one, like Cass, the young woman I met while hiking on a mountain trail.

Cass slumped on her backpack, stuck her feet out over the cliff of the 10,000-foot gorge in the Sierra Nevada, and puffed at me: "So I don't believe the

Bible. There are other religious books, you know."

We still had a 2,000-foot climb into the snow-dotted peaks; I figured she wanted to get into a heavy theological discussion to prolong the rest break. "If God made humans, He's no dummy, right?"

"Right," she said, "If He did."

"Just suppose He did," I said. "If He's intelligent, it would make sense that He'd tell us intelligent beings why He made us, right?"

"I guess so," she allowed.

"So we ought to expect some kind of communique from God. Something that claims to be from God. It would have to be a permanent record of what He says, so every one of us doesn't have to sit and listen to a booming voice in the sky every day. We'd forget fast what He'd said. We'd mistake some of the words. Right?"

"Hmmmm," was all Cass said.

Leaning against my own pack, I explained that there are only three written records that claim to be the truth from God Himself, that all kinds of religious writings exist but that only three state they are directly from God.

She sat up quickly, nearly knocking her water bottle over the edge. "So what are they?"

"The first," I explained, "is the Book of Mormon. I once spent a summer as a missionary to the Mormons in Salt Lake City, and while I was there I examined a first edition copy of the Book of Mormon. On the title page it claims that it was a perfect book when Joseph Smith authored it, yet the Mormons have made over 12,000 changes in it to correct its grammar and doctrinal content. As the Word of God it has some really rough spots. For instance, it reports that God designed a boat but forgot to make any openings in it for the people to enter through or get air to breathe. And with all the recent questions about the book's origin, it's frankly schlockey stuff as an authoritative communique from God."

"What's the second?" she asked.

"The Koran. Interesting stuff — if you're a dedicated male chauvinist," I stated flatly."First," I explained, "Muhammed claimed that he heard the whole thing from the angel Gabriel. Since there were no witnesses, no collaboration from other sources, it makes it very risky to believe that what he was hearing was really from God. Even more of a problem is the fact that heaven is described as a paradise where men can use women to satisfy their every passion. And on earth, women are merely possessions."

Cass had caught on to what this all was leading up to. It was amazing how quickly she decided the "break" was over. Hopping to her feet, she shook her head. "What you say may be true — but I still don't believe the Bible. I just don't like it."

Which is the usual and more honest reason most people refuse to acknowledge the Bible as God's authoritative Word. The Bible doesn't merely contain the Word of God: It *is* the Word of God. This seems like a hair-splitter to some people, but to you and me, it's a vital distinction.

If the Bible only contains the Word of God here and there, you might base half your life on a section that isn't God's truth. If the book isn't the actual Word of God, you wouldn't know which parts are God's truth and which are pure and simple baloney. If the Bible only contains the Word of God, you have no choice but to admit that a life based on the Book is a life founded on guesswork, tradition and experience (see Mark 7:13 and 1 Peter 1:18 on the dangers of the religious tradition).

Stand firm on it: The Bible is inspired, or "breathed out by God" (2 Timothy 3:16).

Hundreds of volumes have been written on the solid authority of the Bible as the Word of God. We certainly don't have time or space to plow through a good study on this crucial topic, so take it on as a project if you haven't already: Study the rationale of the authority and inspiration of the Bible. Two especially good books are Josh McDowell's *Evidence That Demands a Verdict* (San Bernardino, CA: Here's Life Publishers, 1979) and F. F. Bruce's *The New Testament Documents: Are They Reliable?* (Downers Grove, IL: InterVarsity Press, n.d.).

Our English translations are *correct* representations of the original manuscripts of the Bible. With the more than 25,000 handwritten copies of the Bible available to modern scholars, we can be assured that today's translations of God's Word in English are reliable. Still worried about having to rely on a translation instead of the Word in its original languages? Feel free to study Hebrew and Greek, but keep in mind that the New Testament writers frequently quoted from the Greek Septuagint translation of the Hebrew Old Testament. Christ Himself quoted often from the Septuagint version, confirming the validity of accurate translations.

Recent textual research of biblical codices and translations provides fascinating confirmation of the Bible as God's Word. You can get confident about the truth: the Lord's Word is settled forever in heaven (Psalm 119:89), and it's settled right now on earth between the covers of your Bible. It's everything God wants to say to you about His values and their practical outworking in your life.

But even with confidence in the revelation of God's norms, you should be a little uneasy with *law* and *absolutes* as the basis for human rights and wrongs.

The idea of absolutes conjures up at least three basic problems in ethical studies: 1) What happens when these absolute rules conflict? 2) What about the Old Testament laws that God doesn't seem interested in anymore? 3) Absolutism seems to breed crusty legalists who nitpick at life and commit atrocities in the name of Christ as they "go by the book."

When Laws Conflict

God's norms are always tied to overall values. The more specific norms are applications of the more general. For example, the command, "Thou shalt not go faster than 55 m.p.h.," is a specialized statement of "Drive safely," which is an expression of the value the government places on its driving citizenry. "Don't you dare eat two dozen of those chocolate chip cookies" is a specific application under "Don't be a glutton," which is an extension of the higher value of being and feeling healthy.

Because they're interconnected, each level of norms can therefore serve as a "commentary" on the next level. The rationale of a 55 m.p.h. speed limit can be explored by analyzing the principles of safe driving. The value of being healthy explains the ultimate point of not being gluttonous by eating two dozen cookies.

Understanding this gradation of a norm from specific command to principle to basic value is vital to walking away with a clear head from sticky ethical situations in which norms conflict — such as Mrs. Bergmeier's WWII quandary we noted in Chapter Three, or the contemporary issue of abortion. As we'll see shortly, this gradation of norms is a critical element for figuring out the relation between temporary norms and eternal values, *and* for battling the scourge of Christianity — legalism.

Although too much is made of unusual ethical quandaries in which norms conflict, the problem does occur on a small scale. Aunt Ida asks you how she looks in her spandex aerobics outfit; you're to "speak the truth" (Ephesians 4:25) yet how can you and still "be kind" (Ephesians 4:32)? A friend finds she has cancer but wants to conceal it from her family temporarily. You agree not to tell; but when her parents ask you if she's okay — what then?

The Bible has its own examples of situations in which God's norms conflict. The Jewish midwives lied to the ruler of Egypt to protect the lives of newborn boys (Exodus 1:15-22). Rahab lied to protect the Israeli spies (Joshua 2:9-21). Daniel refused to obey his government (Daniel 3 and 6), as did Peter and John (Acts 4:18-19).

Typical responses to the problem of conflicting absolutes include suggesting that the norms themselves do not conflict but the prescribed actions do. Though this concept can explain our feeling of conflict between being kind but not lying to Aunt Ida, it still must deal with such opposites as in Exodus 20:13 and 1 Samuel 15:1-3. Other biblical ethicists suggest we righteously obey one of the conflicting norms and quickly ask forgiveness for the sin of disobeying the other. Both schools' position deserve careful thinking.

However, I think there's a third response to the situation of conflicting laws: You're to respond according to God's ethical hierarchy, which we listed earlier. That is, when norms conflict, — and I believe they can — a norm that embodies a higher value always supercedes or exempts a norm representing a lesser value.

For instance, when the fog rolls through the San Joaquin Valley in central California, and 21-car pile-ups dot Interstate 5, savvy drivers know that the value of remaining a live driver is expressed in the principle, "Drive safely." When good drivers see a mass of swerving taillights through the fog, they putt along well below the 55 m.p.h. maximum and 45 m.p.h. minimum speed limit — although the limits are still definite, absolute laws of the land. Christians are commanded to obey traffic speed limits, norms which embody the value of the government as a representative of God's authority (Romans 13:1-7). But that value is superceded by the value of human life. Drivers are exempted from observing the 45 m.p.h. minimum rule — which is an application of the value of government — when the rule conflicts with a higher rule ("Put on your emergency flashers and drive slowly"), which is an application of the value of life. The 45 m.p.h. minimum is still a law, but it no longer applies when a higher value must be violated to observe it. Think it through: Each of God's commands is absolute in its context of value.

You could spend lifetimes carefully internalizing God's values, such as justice (Isaiah 61:8), dealing truthfully with others (Zechariah 8:16-17), living as earth's visitors whose everlasting home is heaven (Philippians 3:20; 1 Peter 2:11), and so on. Obviously, acknowledging these values in the authoritative Word is good, but adopting God's values through your relationship with Him is what makes biblical ethics "tick" — as we'll soon see. But perhaps you get the idea: It's critical to determine God's values as revealed in His Word.

Is this the ploy of values clarification? Not at all. Values clarification was developed in the '70s as an approach toward moral education by Sidney B. Simon of the University of Massachusetts and Louis E. Raths of the State University of New York, College of Fredonia. The method is simply a model to guide children to choose their own values — regardless of anyone else's values. The premise is that no true values exist, that values are relative. And there's obviously a problem with values clarification: As a system, it has no foundation, no reference point other than the existential preference of the value-clarifier. Of Simon and Raths' seven criteria that must be met for a child to choose a value, the central one is that he be "happy" with it. The deliberation (which is also required in values clarification) and assimilation of values into a lifestyle are admirable steps toward a sensible ethic. But deciding firmly to "do your own thing" isn't much of an improvement over "doing your own thing" with no forethought at all, in my book. So relax, the only values clarifications we're doing is clarifying God's values in our minds.

Another problem Christians may have with the concept of a hierarchy of values is that we are often taught that all norms are valued the same — that breaking one of God's norms is just as bad as breaking any other. This false teaching comes basically from a distortion of James 2:10-11, which actually teaches that when you break any of God's laws, you're a lawbreaker.

However, the fact that God's norms reflect a scale of values is obvious in other instances, such as Jesus' teaching that there are some sins that are worse than others (Matthew 5:22, 12:32, 22:37-38, 23:23); Jesus' prioritizing a "greatest" and a "second" commandment (Matthew 22:37-39); Jesus' statement that there are "weightier provisions of the law" (Matthew 23:23); Jesus' explanation that obeying norms of higher values produces not condemnation but innocence (Matthew 12:1-7); Jesus' assurance to Pilate that the one who delivered Him to Pilate "has the greater sin" (John 19:1); James' warning that because of teachers' influence on others, their conduct "shall incur a stricter judgment" than other Christians' (James 3:1).

When a law representing a lesser value conflicts with a law representing a higher value, you are right to observe the higher-valued law. You are innocent of wrongdoing (see Matthew 12:1-7), since the lower-valued law doesn't apply in a higher-value context.

You notice I keep repeating "when norms conflict." You're never exempt from observing a norm that isn't specifically in conflict with another norm.

For instance, as a Christian, Sam knows he is commanded to follow the norm to "provide for his own, and especially for those of his own household" (1 Timothy 5:8). Sam sells accident insurance, and part of his pitch is a lie. He opens by asking the businessperson, "Did you get the letter sent out about this year's county enrollment?" — which, of course, makes the person ask about the enrollment. Sam knows no letters are ever sent. And it's not a big lie. He justifies it by rationalizing that "lie not" (Colossians 3:9) is superceded by "provide"; besides, he needs to keep his job. But God's style of righteousness is mandatory; Sam needs to be honest in his deliberations. He can provide for his family without lying — even if it takes a job-change, a career-shift, a cross-country move. Nobody ever said righteousness was going to be convenient. So if shifting his sales pitch to observe "lie not" means Sam loses his job, he's just taken the Lord's clear direction for the best possible life. God guides Sam in righteousness, not in rationalization.

Sabbath Days and Tasseled Gowns

I must admit that as a young Christian raised in a conservative atmosphere, I struggled with a kind of ethical "schizophrenia." I boldly proclaimed that I was dead to the law. For example, I knew I was exempt from commands like, "You shall make yourself tassels on the four corners of your garment" (Deuteronomy 22:12). On the other hand, the Ten Commandments were still to be obeyed. Let's clear up this often mushy aspect of understanding God's laws by applying our hierarchical structure.

Norms linked to the *eternal* supercede norms linked to *temporary* values. Colossians 2:16-17 says, "Let no one act as your judge in regard to food or drink or in respect to a festival or a new moon or a Sabbath day — things which are a mere shadow of what is to come; but the substance belongs to Christ". Other passages are equally clear on the temporary, predictive nature of the Old Testament laws: "For the Law, since it is only a shadow of the good things to come and not the very form of things, can never by the same sacrifices year by year . . . make perfect those who draw near. . . Therefore when He comes into the world. . . He takes away the first in order to establish the second" (Hebrews 10:1,5,9).

The temporariness of the Old Testament norms doesn't mean they're without value. The apostle Paul contends that "the Law is holy, and the commandment is holy and righteous and good. . . For we know that the Law is spiritual" (Romans 7:12,14). That's why Jesus didn't break Old Testament laws. He, as the permanent high priest, instead, ushered in a new context — a new covenant. And "when the priesthood is changed, of necessity there takes place a change of law also. For, on the one hand, there is a setting aside of a former commandment because of its weakness and uselessness . . . and on the other hand there is a bringing in of a better hope" (Hebrews 8:12, 18-19). Old covenant priests "served a copy and shadow of the heavenly things" (Hebrews 8:5); but "when (God) said, 'A new covenant,' He had made the first obsolete" (Hebrews 8:13). These Mosaic laws, "regulations . . imposed until a time of reformation" (Hebrews 9:10), a "ministry of death in letters engraved on stones" (2 Corinthians 3:7), are superceded by new covenant norms.

Let's take my fairly innocuous Sabbath/Sunday conflict — a controversy that throws some Christians: If Saturday is the Sabbath, why do most Christians worship on Sunday? "Remember the Sabbath day, to keep it holy" (Exodus 20:8-11) was enforced to the letter by Moses. An Israelite was stoned to death for picking up sticks on the Sabbath (Numbers 15:32-36; see Exodus 31:14).

But Jesus announced a new covenant: "The Sabbath was made for man, and not man for the Sabbath. Consequently, the Son of Man is Lord even of the Sabbath" (Mark 2:27-28). And after Christ's death on the cross — the pivotal point between the two covenants — Paul described the basics of the norm which supercedes: "Now that you have come to know God . . . how is it that you turn your back again to the weak and worthless elemental things, to which you desire to be enslaved all over again? You observe days and months and seasons and years (of the Jewish Holy days)" (Galatians 4:9-11). The permanent value illustrated in Sabbatical law is the *rest from works* enjoyed by believers: "We who have believed enter that rest. . . There remains therefore a Sabbath rest for the people of God. For the one who has entered His rest has himself also rested from his works, as God did from His" (Hebrews 4:1-11). Resting in faith is the spiritual value that stood behind the letter of the law all along.

There is no command anywhere in the New Testament that reinstates the Sabbath as a New Covenant observance. New Covenant believers are exempted from observing the temporary law of the Sabbath that was given to Israel; we're now obligated to focus on the eternal value, the permanent meaning of the Sabbath.

However, before we close on this issue, let's be clear: Norms connected to New Covenant, eternal values supercede conflicting norms connected to Old Covenant, temporary values. Most of the superceded Old Covenant norms, you'll find, are Jewish civil and ceremonial rules. An Old Testament law *does* apply if it's repeated explicitly or implicitly in the New Testament. When there is no conflict of norms, no exemption is allowed since God's norms are eternal (Isaiah 40:8). Violating an eternal norm is sin, and sin brings consequences: "Do not be deceived, God is not mocked; for whatever a man sows, this he will also reap. For the one who sows to his own flesh shall from the flesh reap corruption" (Galatians 6:7-8). Does Paul here sound like a dreaded legalist? We'll look at that problem in the next chapter.

But for now, if you sense the panic rising in you that this is just another rule book or that we're fast falling from grace when we focus on God's norms, relax. If you'll allow the Spirit to renew your way of looking at God's norms in the whole context of His ethical system, you'll soon be meditating along with King David:

The law of the Lord is perfect, restoring the soul;

The testimony of the Lord is sure, making wise the simple;

The precepts of the Lord are right, rejoicing the heart;

The commandment of the Lord is pure, enlightening the eyes.

The fear of the Lord is clean, enduring forever;

The judgments of the Lord are true; they are righteous altogether.

They are more desirable than gold, yes, than much fine gold;

Sweeter also than honey and the drippings of the honeycomb (Psalm 19:7-10).

For Study, Thought and Discussion

Think through these passages:

Exodus 20:3-4; Acts 5:27-29

Genesis 1:26-27; Exodus 21:22-25; Matthew 6:26; 12:11-12

Matthew 25:32-46

Joshua 2 with Hebrews 11:31 and James 2:25

Deuteronomy 23:21-23; Matthew 5:37; James 5:12

Notice the order of creation in Genesis 1.

Matthew 6:31-33; John 6:63; 1 Timothy 4:7-8

2 Corinthians 4:18; Colossians 2:16-17; Hebrews 9:11-15; 10:1-14

Then prioritize according to God's values. . .
— inanimate non-living matter
— a finite person able and willing to contribute to the personhood* of others
— several finite persons
— a finite person unable or unwilling to contribute to the personhood of others
— an infinite person
— a finite person's vow
— action that contributes temporarily to personhood
— animated matter
— action that contributes eternally to personhood
— action that doesn't necessarily contribute to personhood
*Consider "personhood" as the process of a person becoming all a human can be.

Sort through the concept of ethical hierarchy by noting the value-status of the conflicting norms involved in these sticky-ethics situations:

— When the Gestapo asks where the Jews are hiding, according to God's values, which norm — lying or participating in the murder — supercedes which?

— How could Abraham or Saul even consider obeying God's directions to them? (See Exodus 20:13; Genesis 22:1-19 and 1 Samuel 15:1-3.)

— When either an unborn baby or a mother must die, what order of values exempts a doctor from a charge of murder?

— Why was Jephthah's sacrifice of his daughter wrong (Judges 11:30-40)?

— If suicide is an act of murdering one's self, what about the soldier who jumps on a live grenade in a crowded foxhole?

— Did God violate His own laws in Acts 10:9-16? (See also Deuteronomy 14:4-20.)

— What do you do as the ranking officer of the overloaded lifeboat that's about to sink?

— Why was Rahab, the lying prostitute, praised as an example of faith (Hebrews 11:31; James 2:25)?

— What do you think about capital punishment as it conflicts with the premeditated killing of a human being?

— What about the conflicting rules in a situation of protecting your family from a killer?

— Is the concept of hierarchical values any help in determining your actions if you'd been in Mrs. Bergmeier's shoes?

5
Laws and Legalism

We have probably all seen our share of instances wherein Christians who base their "biblical ethics" solely on the foundation of law have fallen into suffocating legalism. It's remarkable that legalism still thrives among Christians when the New Testament so firmly curses it (Matthew 23; 1 Timothy 4:1-4).

Francis Schaeffer, in *True Spirituality*, warned:

> Often, after a person is born again, and asks "What shall I do next?" he is given a list of things usually of a limited nature, and primarily negative. Often he is given the idea that if he does not do this series of things (whatever this series of things happens to be in the particular country and location and at the time he happens to live), he will be spiritual. This is not so. . . . We still must emphasize that the Christian life, or true spirituality, is more than refraining from a certain external list of taboos in a mechanical way.[1]

What's the nature of the beast of legalism? Legalism is forming your own canon of authoritative laws: Make up your own godly-sounding rule and announce "Thus saith the Lord" about it. Do I need to list examples of this phase of the disease? How many times has "the name of God been blasphemed" among non-Christians because of pompous Christians who push their own opinions as God's laws? (See Romans 2:17-24.)

Paul warned the Colossians, "See to it that no one takes you captive through philosophy and empty deception, according to the tradition of men, according to the elementary principles of the world, rather than according to Christ" (Colossians 2:8).

Another type of legalism is claiming that your application of God's norms is inspired and authoritative. The Jewish Pharisees mastered the art of authoritatively augmenting, "explaining" and illustrating the how-to's of Mosaic laws. For instance, one of their Talmudic guidelines for "remembering the Sabbath to keep it holy" allowed drinking vinegar to soothe a sore throat; but gargling the vinegar was grounds for stoning.

Legalism can also mean ignoring the biblical norms you don't like. It's the kind of Pharisaical hypocrisy Jesus railed at:

> "You tithe mint and dill and cummin, and have neglected the weightier provisions of the law; justice and mercy and faithfulness; but these are the things you should have done without neglecting the others" (Matthew 23:23).

Since it's easy to fool some of the people some of the time, legalism focuses on following codes of external behavior — the kind of righteousness that impresses people (Matthew 6:1-5; Romans 4:2) who look on the outward appearance rather than the heart (1 Samuel

16:7). Since acting is easier than being, a good legalist acts out the easier norms and ignores the inner, tougher ones. Legalists polish the outside of the cup, but "inside they are full of robbery and self-indulgence" (Matthew 23:26). They're like "whitewashed tombs which on the outside appear beautiful, but inside they are full of dead men's bones and all uncleanness. (They) outwardly appear righteous to men, but inwardly . . . are full of hypocrisy and lawlessness" (Matthew 23:27-28).

Legalism is trying to fulfill God's norms under old-nature power. Trying to obey God is excruciatingly frustrating to the non-believer who's trapped in the old nature, and to the believer who because of unconfessed sin is walking in the old nature. Old-nature righteousness, even when it's sincere, is like a pile of greasy rags (Isaiah 64:6) that are useless for cleaning up anyone.

Legalism preaches that by sticking to the rules you can clean up your act enough to be saved from hell for heaven, and you can become a better Christian. But Paul tells the Galatians, "Knowing that a man is not justified by the works of the law but through faith in Christ Jesus, even we have believed in Christ Jesus, that we may be justified by faith in Christ, and not by the works of the law; since by the works of the law shall no flesh be justified" (Galatians 2:16).

Now we're talking about the more subtle game of legalism — sanctification or justification by works — becoming a better Christian by doing good things. And that's a much more touchy issue.

I am assuming that, at some point in your life, you have made a commitment to Jesus Christ and trusted Him for your salvation. (If your assurance of that decision is in the least bit fuzzy, it's time to recheck your understanding of the Bible's teaching on salvation: Think through John 17:3; 1 Peter 5:10; Romans 3:23;

6:23; 5:6-8; 1 John 2:2; 2 Corinthians 5:15,21; Ephesians 2:8-9; Revelation 3:20; Romans 10:9-10.)

Sanctification/Justification by Works: A Fallacy

Now let's look at the implications of this salvation as it relates to God's rules and laws.

The Mosaic Law, and all God's laws, describe a perfect human, who, of course, wouldn't need to be "saved" to enter God's perfection: "The doers of the law (literally "of Law") will be justified" (Romans 2:13). However, we know that all humans are dead (separated from God's life) "in trespasses and sins" (Ephesians 2:1). So God's norms only point out our inability to save ourselves — stuck as we are in our dead old nature, "the flesh."

Haven't we all at some time joined the ranks of the courageous though pathetic people who, under their own steam, are trying to live a righteous life? Urging old-nature-powered people to live in righteousness is like shouting "Everybody dance!" in a cemetery.

God's commandments, "which were to result in life" (Romans 7:10), and which are "spiritual," only prove "I am of flesh, sold into bondage to sin" (Romans 7:14). Shouting "dance!" to a dead body only emphasizes the deadness. The law — God's standards — never sanctifies, never justifies, never gives life. The only effect of the law on sin-natured humans is a curse of condemnation (Galatians 3:10-13). Law's reign is called a "ministry of death" (2 Corinthians 3:9).

Yet Christ fulfilled the law (Matthew 5:17), and so He is not condemned by it. Believers have "clothed" themselves with this perfect Christ "through faith" (Galatians 3:26,27). So "there is therefore now no condemnation to those who are in Christ Jesus" (Romans 8:1). The legal requirement — "The wages of sin is death" (Romans 6:23) — is suspended when we participate by faith in Christ's New Covenant. By faith, we are dead to the power of the law, free from its condemnation (Romans 6:3-7; 7:1-6; Galatians 5:1). Paul pointedly emphasizes this in his anti-legalistic letter to the Galatians: "If a law had been given which was able to impart life, then righteousness would indeed have been based on law. But the Scripture has shut up all men under sin, that the promise by faith in Jesus Christ might be given to those who believe" (Galatians 3:21-22).

The law *is* perfect. But a legalistic case for salvation is absurd, since law does nothing for a dead, sin nature except emphasize its deadness. The apostle Paul boasted that he would be found blameless if anyone were to examine him according "to the righteousness which is in the law." But he concluded, "I count all things to be loss in view of the surpassing value of knowing Christ Jesus my Lord . . . not having a righteousness of my own derived from the law, but that which is through faith in Christ, the righteousness which comes from God on the basis of faith" (Philippians 3:6,8,9).

Sanctification/Justification by Faith: The Truth

So how *do* I become "a better Christian"?

The answer to that question is: through sanctification, that is, the process of being "set apart" from sin, set apart to Him. We are told to "pursue sanctification" (Hebrews 12:14). "As you therefore have received Christ Jesus the Lord," Paul writes to the church at Colosse, "so walk in Him" (Colossians 2:6). It should be fairly obvious that, since we received Christ by faith (Ephesians 2:8,9), we're also then to grow away from sin and toward Him by faith (Acts 26:18).

The Spirit shapes us to become like God by helping us think through and by faith adopt truth — God's values in His Word. Notice the following verses: "Do not be conformed to this world, but be transformed by the renewing of your mind" (Romans 12:2); "Be renewed in the spirit of your mind, and put on the new self, which in the likeness of God has been created in righteousness and holiness of the truth" (Ephesians 4:23,24).

To the believer growing to be like God, the norms aren't written on tablets of stone anymore. And they're not simply for cursory, brain-level acknowledgment. God's laws are now to be found etched in our hearts (Romans 1:19ff, 2:14ff, 2 Corinthians 3:2-8). We're to concentrate on the meanings — the "spirit" — of the law, not the old letters (Jeremiah 31:33, Romans 7:6). The Spirit uses what we have, and He's very interested that what we have in the heart — not just the brain — is God's eternal truth: "Behold, Thou dost desire truth in the innermost being, and in the hidden part Thou wilt make me know wisdom" (Psalm 51:6, KJV).

Transforming Renewal

Let's look more closely at that renewing process to avoid crossing over into the legalistic mindset that says, "Do the rules to be godly."

Under Spirit control, your mind and heart soak up a truth, a value-statement of God's Word. The Spirit uses that truth to renew your mind as you decide to begin thinking and feeling and prioritizing that value the way God does. In the process, when your Spirit-led will activates a renewed thought/feeling/value, you will act in accordance with divine norms — according to "the law of the Spirit of life" (Romans 8:2), "the perfect law, the law of liberty" (James 1:25). Truth-by-truth, you become more like Christ.

This isn't one of those which-comes-first chicken or egg games of semantics. Stepping into your new nature under the control of the Spirit is first. Acting out God's standards is second. Doing the second without the first is legalism.

Rule-keeping focuses on the body acting in accordance with God's norms; sanctification involves the whole body-soul-spirit person adopting God's norms — with the body being the least significant participant. Rule-keeping focuses on the rules; sanctification involves understanding the rules as statements of God's values. Rule-keeping can flounder along even when a person's old sin nature is the controlling force; sanctification happens only through the transforming power of the Spirit. Rule-keeping is a futile, teeth-gritting attempt to be righteous in practice by doing certain works and not doing others; sanctification is the Spirit-led and therefore spiritual process of trusting what God has said about living by faith, since "the righteous one shall live by faith"! (Habbakuk 2:4; Romans 1:17; Galatians 3:11; Hebrews 10:38)

Here's a little test to check the solidity of your perspective on the place of biblical norms in the Spirit-led believer's life. Re-read the following passage from 1 John, which we first discussed regarding obedience to God's commands. See if you now can cross the fine line between regarding those commands as burdensome rules as things we have to try to do, or as statements of our becoming godly by faith, of thinking like God, of adopting God's values as our own values:

> By this we know that we have come to know Him, if we keep His commandments. . . . Whoever keeps His word, in him the love of God has truly been perfected. . . . Whatever we ask we receive from Him, because we keep His commandments and do the things that are pleasing in His sight. . . . By this we know that we love the children of God, when we love God and observe His commandments. For this is the love of God, that we keep His commandments; and His commandments are not burdensome.

The implications of how it all fits together — why God created us, of our becoming like Him, of sin and law and salvation and obeying the requirements of God's norms by the Spirit — are sometimes so mind-boggling that we need to snap our thinking back to the simple statements of the truth:

> There is therefore now no condemnation for those who are in Christ Jesus. For the law of the Spirit of life in Christ Jesus has set you free from the law of sin and death. For what the law could not do, weak as it was through the flesh, God did: sending His own Son in the likeness of sinful flesh and as an offering for sin, He condemned sin in the flesh, in order that the requirement of the law might be fulfilled in us who do not walk according to the flesh, but according to the Spirit (Romans 8:1-4).

Let's recap some of the key points we've discussed regarding God's law being a prime ingredient in the biblical system of ethics:

- God's norms — principles and commands — are absolute.
- Our applications or conclusions on how to use God's norms aren't absolute.
- When these absolute norms conflict, God's hierarchical scale of values dictates which norm is suspended within that context.
- New Testament believers are exempted, then, from observing Old Testament laws such as civil and ceremonial norms.
- New Testament believers are free from the penalty but not necessarily the practical consequences of breaking God's norms.
- Never intended as methods of justification or sanctification, God's norms are still to be assimi-

lated as indications of God's nature, of how God thinks.

- As the Spirit transforms us to value what God values, we'll more and more fulfill God's norms since they'll become our norms.
- Practical righteousness — right living — is possible with Spirit control and truth from the Word. Did I say "possible"? Let's get accurate: Practical righteousness is mandatory! (Romans 7:4; Ephesians 2:10; 2 Timothy 2:21; 3:16)

Are you still leery of all this talk about laws and norms, threatened by the specter of legalism? Let's get an even more balanced perspective of God's system of living right by thinking through a second element: love.

For Study, Thought and Discussion

Read Romans 7 and 8. In what major areas of your life do you feel you still need work?

Focus in on Romans 8:9,10. What gives you the power to become righteous? What does God say about you the way you are right now?

By what process do you become like God? Read Galatians 4:19; 2 Corinthians 3:18.

As righteousness pervades your soul, what is the external result? Frame your thoughts or discussion around 1 Thessalonians 5:23 and Romans 6:9. How do these verses relate to your idea of "piety"?

6
Love Is

Love is the essence and the substance of right living.

But why should you be loved? I'd really like you to answer the question. Look away from the book and spend a few minutes to come up with your answer.

Keeping that answer in mind, imagine yourself suddenly struck with a horrible but temporary disease. You shrivel, you slip in and out of consciousness and are hospitalized as a virtual vegetable for the next six years. Here's my next question: Should you still be loved for the same reasons?

Regardless of your answer for the first question, I hope you came up with a definite yes for the second. Those qualities that deserve admiration, those abilities that are valuable, those unique touches that are you are only latent when you're unconscious. The potential is always there. You and every human deserve to be loved — to be admired and cared for and valued — because of the human potential to reflect the most admirable, most deserving, most valued Being in the universe: You are imprinted with the image of God (Genesis 1:26-27). The implications of this simple fact are monumental in our development of a God-centered system of right and wrong in which love is the key.

Remember the first time you fell madly in love? Let's say you had ridden your little sister's "Smurf" bike down to the ice cream parlor for an afternoon fix. You were in cutoff Levi's and a gray, ripped-up T-shirt that said "My Parents Went to Detroit and All They Brought Me Was This Lousy T-Shirt" — now it had a mud stripe up the back from riding through puddles. Throwing open the door at the ice cream parlor, you suddenly came face-to-face with the most gorgeous thing you had ever laid eyes on. You mumbled as you held the door open, "Uh, like my shirt?" The gorgeous thing attempted a smile and promptly walked out of your life.

You spent the next four days making up conversations in your head: "If only I'd said the right thing! If only I'd been wearing the right outfit!"

You and I still do it: In our moments of infatuation, in our days of falling in love, in our years of being in love, we want to say and do the right things, dress right, look right, be right for the sake of the beloved. And that should tell us something profound about right living.

Love is a powerful motivator. Consequently, situation ethics (discussed briefly in Chapter Three) is an admirable human attempt at living the best possible life, since the essence of situation ethics is to choose what is loving. Love is "the fulfillment of the whole law" (Romans 13:10). But trying to live on the basis of human love is risky business, because most of us know that, as a book by Lewis Grizzard puts it, *If Love Was Oil, I'd Be About A Quart Low.*

All You Need Is Love

I'll never forget my reflection in the Eugene, Oregon, airport windows on a summer day in 1969: I was a shiny skinhead in Army dress greens. I'd flown out to visit a sister at the famous laid-back farm of counter-culture guru, Ken Kesey. I knew I would not fit in.

Wonderful people meandered about the farm, and, once I traded my dress greens for blue jeans, I guess they took my shaved head as the sign of an eastern-religious type. Everybody seemed to want to talk religion and love.

"I live by love," the young guy with glazed black eyes nodded, sitting on a hay bale between practice sets of a visiting band. "We all do around here. See, if I love my girl, I won't do anything to hurt her, right? If I love my dogs, I'll be good to 'em. If I love myself, I'll take care of by body and brain. If I love you — ." He paused.

I shifted uneasily. But not because the guy wasn't on the right track. Living by love *would* produce a righteous life.

> Owe nothing to anyone except to love one another, for he who loves his neighbor has fulfilled the law. For this, "You shall not commit adultery, you shall not murder, you shall not steal, you shall not covet," and if there is any other commandment, it is summed up in this saying, "You shall love your neighbor as yourself." Love does no wrong to a neighbor; love therefore is the fulfillment of the law (Romans 13:8-10).

"Wow, man." I tried to sound eastern-religious and laid-back. "But what's love?"

He pulled out a pouch and a packet of cigarette papers and explained caring and meeting needs and giving pleasure.

"Yeah," I interjected, "but tell me — do you always love other people — all of them? For instance, if I were a guy in the Army being trained for Viet Nam — ."

"I'd slice you up and feed you to the hogs," he said.

"Right. And how about yourself? Do you always love yourself perfectly?" (And I guess I should have followed up with an ultimate: "Do you always love God perfectly?")

He shrugged. And at that moment — I could not believe the timing — two of the commune kids scrabbled around the side of the barn, screaming and beating the pie out of each other. Within moments, the mothers were involved, glaring and taunting each other and the kids. Soon a few men came out. One slapped a kid, then the others started shoving the man who did the slapping.

I looked at my friend.

"Hey-y-y-y," he grinned. "We're only human."

Is not knowing how to love and not practicing love just the problem of dope smokers? Wake up and smell the smog: Even Bible-thumping Christians — God's representatives of righteousness — snarl and gossip and shake fists at each other (and, secretly, at God). Have you been to a denominational convention lately when a controversial issue was raised? Although "the love of God has been poured out within our hearts" (Romans 5:5), we Christians rarely seem to appropriate our ability to love. We're all "only human."

Being human puts us all at a distinct disadvantage. One of the basics of God's style of love is a self-giving attitude (John 3:16; 15:13), and that's the last thing an old-sin-nature self wants to have. Especially in the middle of Bonhoeffer's "unique and transient situations," we're not very good at applying the norm of love. We're all subject to manipulation by our old natures, and no one consistently does good — "not even one" (Romans 3:10-12).

Problems in applying love stem naturally from a more basic problem: We're not very good at knowing what love is.

What Is Love, Anyway?

Agape is God's norm of love. The Greek verb *agapao* is distinctly characteristic of Christianity; its use in the New Testament was unprecedented in classical Greek literature as well as the Septuagint. Since the word expresses the essential nature of God — "God is agape" (1 John 4:8) — you can be sure we'll never completely understand the term. God's style of love, according to *Vine's Expository Dictionary of New Testament Words,* is thoroughly selfless. It is "not drawn out by any excellency in its objects (Romans 5:8). It was an exercise of the divine will in deliberate choice, made without assignable cause save that which lies in the nature of God Himself. Christian love . . . is not an impulse from the feelings, it does not always run with the natural inclinations, nor does it spend itself only upon those for whom some affinity is discovered."

Carson McCullers authored the short story, "A Tree. A Rock. A Cloud." which I used to teach every semester in a college literature class. In the story, an old man, a middle-aged man and a boy realize they don't know anything about love. And yet the first thing they try to do with this strange feeling is to love a woman. And the results are sad, to say the least. McCuller's suggestion is that men try to learn to love simply at first, to appreciate a tree for what it is, a rock for itself, a cloud for simply being a cloud — not for what these things can "do" to a man.

As the class discussed this point, I'd ask, "What do you think, ladies? Would you like to be loved simply for being you — not for how much pleasure you could give a guy or for how proud you make him feel to be seen with you or for how desirable you could make yourself?" Invariably the classroom would be deathly still. Then I'd ask the guys: "Wouldn't it be something if you didn't have to try to impress a girl with your brains or your muscles or size or how much money you make or will make? If she'd just love you thoroughly — just for who you are?" Especially during those desperate college-age years of helter-skelter love relationships, the disparity between typical human love and the genuine article is downright sad.

Valuing, admiring, caring for someone simply for who that person *is* is God's kind of love. Love is fulfilling God's commands in action and attitude. God clearly tells us that real love isn't a feeling at all; it's something you can choose: "For this is the love of God, that we keep His commandments" (1 John 5:3); "And this is love, that we walk in obedience to His commands" (2 John 6, NIV).

You can choose to love. Otherwise it would make no sense to be commanded to love: "Love your neighbor" (Leviticus 19:18); "Love the Lord your God" (Deuteronomy 6:5); "Show love for the stranger" (Deuteronomy 10:19); "I command you today to love the Lord" (Deuteronomy 30:16); "Take diligent heed to love the Lord" (Joshua 23:11); "Love truth and peace" (Zechariah 8:19); "Love your enemies" (Matthew 5:44); "Husbands, love your wives" (Ephesians 5:25); "Encourage the young women to love their husbands, to love their children" (Titus 2:4); "Love one another" (1 Peter 1:22); "Love the brotherhood" (1 Peter 2:17); "Do not love the world" (1 John 2:15). Agape must be something we can choose or not choose. It's not an emotional entity that is "in the air" waiting to zap an arrow through your heart when it "hits you."

Feelings of attraction, compassion, admiration, desire and mutual dependence are all right. They're enjoyable, and they often accompany love. But feelings are not love itself — at least not the love described by God in 1 Corinthians 13: Real love is patient, kind, not jealous; it doesn't brag, isn't arrogant, doesn't act unbecomingly, doesn't seek its own, isn't provoked, doesn't carry grudges, rejoices with the truth but not in unrighteousness; bears and endures the worst; believes and hopes the best; and never quits. Love isn't a feeling; it's a pattern of fulfilling God's commands in action and attitude.

The fact that love isn't a feeling is a good guideline to hold on to, since strong feelings that are mistaken for love can lead you into some incredibly frustrating, dangerous and foolish "love" relationships and out of some real love relationships. You can feel the feelings of "falling in love" with many people. You can be strongly, romantically attracted even to a person who is wrong for you. You can be infatuated for months, only to eventually find after you get to know the person that you really don't like him or her at all. You can rationalize destructive relationships with, "It must be right. We can't deny what we feel!"

Yes, you can. And sometimes you must. A couple fooled into thinking love is a warm, racy feeling can marry on the basis of that feeling; then when the feelings fade they think: "Love is gone. I must have married the wrong one." Or a person who confuses wonderful romance with real love might marry, then years later find he or she is wildly attracted to someone else. The thought "He/she makes me feel those old feelings again!" is the basis of tens of thousands of real-life soap operas.

Racy and romantic and wonderful feelings are good; God designed men and women to be attracted to each other. The couple keeps seeing each other because the two of them feel so fantastic whenever they're together. It feels good, and it is good. But real love — the pattern of thinking about and treating others the way God would — needs to take root and grow to carry the couple through the inevitable times when they're not feeling so fantastic. I hope it's as comforting to you as it is to me: Real love can flourish regardless of feelings.

Loving Is A Process

Since loving God, others and yourself properly is the essence of right living, and since love isn't a feeling, you don't have to conjure up wonderful feelings for humankind or passionate rapture about yourself or infatuation for God in order to love properly. Rather, God has given us guidelines on how to love in perfect justice and purity. Look again at the apostle John's definition: "Loving God means obeying His commands, and these commands are not burdensome" (1 John 5:3, Phillips). He writes again that "real love means obeying the Father's orders, and you have known from the beginning that you must live in obedience to Him" (2 John 5, Phillips).

Think it through: God's commands involve all three areas of relationship — to God, others, and to self (which just happen to incorporate every possible situation in a human life). When God commands, "You shall have no other gods before Me" (Exodus 20:3), it's a prescription for loving Him properly. "Give preference to one another in honor" gives us a basic on loving others (Romans 12:10). He says one way of loving ourselves properly is to "set (our) minds on the things above" (Colossians 3:2). Knowing perfectly well how thick-headed we can be, God has given us a complete set of practical, explicit and implicit guidelines on loving properly in all three types of relationships. These are not rules for rules' sake; these are norms that, as we internalize the values they represent, describe our relationships of love.

Are you catching onto the almost maddening circularity of love and law? Consider Jesus' statements: "If you love Me, you will keep My commandments"; "He who has My commandments and keeps them, he it is who loves Me" (John 14:15,21). Living righteously demands love, and love is delineated by God's law, and law is fulfilled by love!

Law and love are both emanations of who God is. God's norms describe God's love. Love isn't a separate, "special" norm; it's the substance of all norms — it's the fulfillment of the law.

Back To Basics

Now that we've defined what love is, we're back to the old question: "How can I live according to God's norms and love with God's agape love?"

The process is exactly like the justification and sanctification by faith we discussed in the last chapter. In salvation you were given a divine, new nature in which you can walk day by day under the control of the Holy Spirit. The Spirit guides you into all truth in God's Word. As you decide — truth by truth — to believe, to adopt God's thoughts, you think more and more as He does. The Spirit uses your renewed thinking to transform you. You begin to know God for who He is, not for what He does. Your values shift to mimic His values. In your innermost being — not on a brain-level but in your mind and heart — you begin to see the infinite value of others and the inestimable value of yourself as God sees you. As you think in your heart, so you'll be (Proverbs 23:7).

The apostle Peter describes the process of love-by-sanctification in a way that demands slow, thoughtful reading:

> Since you have in obedience to the truth purified
> your souls for a sincere love of the brethren, fer-

vently love one another from a clean heart, for
you have been born again not of seed which is
perishable but imperishable, that is, through the
living and abiding word of God (1 Peter 1:22-23).

Of course, you're free to decide not to love. If you
decide to slide back into your old nature, to love
yourself in the lust of the flesh and of the eyes and
in the boastful pride of life, the love of the Father will
not be "passing through" you (1 John 2:15-16). The
presence of the Holy Spirit is your personal resource
for *agape*. When He entered you, He poured out love
in your heart (Romans 5:5); He created your new nature
in the image of God (Ephesians 4:24), who is love (1
John 4:8).

But you *can* live out the pattern of becoming conformed to God's image as a life-style of right loving.
Or you can think of it as a pattern of right living. The
love of Christ will control you (literally, "press" or
"urge" you) to live no longer for yourself. You'll value
or "recognize no man according to the flesh," according
to human values, but according to his potential as "a
new creature in Christ." Treating people according to
those values will earn you the reputation of being an
ambassador for Christ, because you are actually becoming "the righteousness of God" (2 Corinthians 5:14-
17,20-21). Attitudes and actions of love are synonymous
with righteousness. Love will grow in you:

> . . . in real knowledge and discernment, so that
> you may approve the things that are excellent, in
> order to be sincere and blameless until the day
> of Christ, having been filled with the fruit of
> righteousness which comes through Jesus Christ
> (Philippians 1:9-10).

And you will:

> . . . increase and abound in love for one another,
> and for all men . . . so that He may establish
> your hearts unblamable in holiness before our
> God (1 Thessalonians 3:12).

Right living requires right loving; and loving requires choice. And choice requires the third essential: freedom.

For Study, Thought and Discussion

Read Matthew 22:34-40. Consider and discuss God's priority-scale for loving. Is it essential that we love in that order? Why?

Read Luke 9:57-62. Discuss Jesus' response to the three disciples.

Read John 13:4-16. Consider the different areas of your life (work, school, marriage, etc.) and any difficulties you may be experiencing in loving. In light of Jesus' example, how can you specifically begin to love when those relationships get rocky?

7

Freedom's Not Just Another Word

A kid on a retreat lies back on his bunk and tells me, "Freedom is gettin' to do what I want, with whoever I want."

"Freedom", suggests Robert Frost in his poetry, is "working easy in the harness."

"Freedom," sings Janis Joplin, "is just another word for nothin' left to lose."

"Freedom," writes Jacques Ellul in *The Ethics of Freedom,* "is never comfortable."

Freedom's a slippery item to win, to hang onto, even to define. But misunderstanding Christian freedom is a killer to understanding biblical rights and wrongs. Freedom is the milieu of true ethics. In fact, the whole scheme of wrong and right would be meaningless without actual, down-to-earth freedom.

Are We Free To Choose?

Can we be genuinely free?

Theologians and philosophers alike have toyed for centuries with the thought that man is never truly free, that he and his every action are determined by the ticking mechanics of a closed system of cause and effect. Man can pretend he's free, but his choices are only illusory. Nietzsche held that the determinism of the universe spun cycles of recurring happenings to be endured again and again by pathetic man. Tom Robbins in *Even Cowgirls Get The Blues* parodies a classic philosophical horror story on Nietzsche's theme:

> For Christmas that year, Julian gave Sissy a miniature Tyrolean village. The craftsmanship was remarkable.
> There was a tiny cathedral whose stained-glass windows made fruit salad of sunlight. There was a plaza and *ein Biergarten*. The *Biergarten* got quite noisy on Saturday nights. There was a bakery that smelled always of hot bread and strudel. There was a town hall and a police station, with cutaway sections that revealed standard amounts of red tape and corruption. There were little Tyroleans in leather britches, intricately stitched. There were ski shops and many other interesting things, including an orphanage. The orphanage was designed to catch fire and burn down every Christmas Eve. Orphans would dash into the snow with their nightgowns blazing. Terrible. Around the second week of January, a fire inspector would come and poke through the ruins, muttering, "If they had only listened to me, those children would be alive today."[1]

The Stoics preached this style of terrible, choiceless determinism. They held that man had only as much "free" choice as a dog tied to a wagon. He can choose to resist the pull of the wagon called Fate, or he can choose to follow where he's led and pretend the usually miserable destination was his own idea all along.

Determinism leans toward despair. According to Wittgenstein, we have no more freedom than autumn leaves floating to the ground, saying to themselves, "Now I think I'll go this way. . . Now that way."[2] Determinism still flourishes, despite discoveries in fields as diverse as psychology or physics. Scientists are finding that cause-and-effect is not the governing principle of the universe. Many of today's agnostic thinkers, drawing from physics, engineering, automata theory, artificial intelligence, and even evolutionary theory conclude that man is a being with a free will.

Philosophy professor Daniel Dennett of Tufts University suggests that today's free will problem is not with philosophical determinism, it's with a scientific mindset which feels driven to quantify everything in the universe. Dennett writes, "What we want when we want free will is the power to decide our courses of action, and to decide them wisely, in the light of our expectations and desires. . . We want to be agents capable of initiating and taking responsibility for projects and deeds...We are afraid that science has shown or will soon show that we can't be what we want to be. The threat is not determinism — if it were, we could all relax, since physicists now seem to agree that our world is fundamentally indeterministic — but science itself, or the 'naturalism' that is its enabling world view."[3]

Unfortunately, many Christians struggle with a deterministic mindset, confused about the doctrine of the sovereignty of God. God *is* sovereign. Yet, again and again in Scripture, man is presented as a creature who can choose to violate or agree to God's norms.

Think through the apparently undetermined season of the Abomination of Desolation in Matthew 24:20; the "by coincidence" of Luke 10:31; God's "repenting of the evil He would do" in Exodus 32:14; the "whosoever will" of John 3:16 and Revelation 3:20; the fact that God holds man responsible for choosing to obey or disobey His norms (see Hebrews 2:2). God holds us accountable, and that tells us that we can choose, that we have free wills.

As humans, our most important choice focuses on Christ's redemptive work on the cross.

And I won't even bother getting into the existence of evil as the most vivid proof that God allows freedom of choice.

We're free to choose. That fact is obviously important when it comes to rationalizing wrong attitudes or actions. It's easy to think we really had no choice; our response was forced on us by cosmic forces or a snarling aunt, or poverty, or the devil, or our glands. But real freedom is more than simply having a choice, it's having the ability to carry out the choice, and to feel free doing it!

Feeling Free

Would you like to feel free? Free from that upcoming term paper, assigned arbitrarily by a professor for an arbitrary date on an arbitrary subject putting arbitrary pressure on you? Do you want to be free from obligations like having to wash the car, phone Mother, love your spouse, change diapers, watch your weight, pay taxes for the latest anti-ballistic missile, smile at the boss, go to church, brush your teeth, limit your sexual exploits?

The kind of liberty that's necessary for a solid ethical system is the same kind of liberty that can actually free you from the squeeze of the restrictions we just listed. The problem, however, is that churches aren't renowned as paragons of freedom. Born-again believers are often viewed — and often rightly — as repressed, cookie-cutter conformists who actually fear freedom! So it's critical that we get a good handle on both personal and ecclesiastical freedom. Let's look first at what freedom isn't; then at what it is.

Dream Freedom

The "Doors' " late Jim Morrison characterized the "dream freedom" life-style of the late '60s with his statement, "We want the world and we want it now!" Having everything we want, with no rules, limitations, or obligations — that's the kind of freedom we sometimes dream about. It's the no-laws utopia of antinomianism. But it is just a dream. Real life can't operate without laws.

The universe is coded with natural laws and principles. Gravity as a phenomenon of the space-time continuum is necessary; a recent study of space rats verified that weightlessness develops a weak tissue structure, and humans in space will need to maintain artificial gravity in order to experience proper physiological growth and function. Personal restrictions are necessary. Getting stone-drunk and paying for it with DWI's and serious headaches will probably lead to a personal code of "I guess I won't drink so much anymore."

Face it, when you have a deep desire to go into business, in reality the first thing you want is expert advice on the laws of incorporating and investing. When you-want to impress someone, you follow the rules of courtesy. A love relationship demands that you follow the guidelines of interpersonal relationships.

The point is this: Dream freedom — which doesn't exist — isn't what we really want anyway.

False Freedom

Dream freedom may not exist, but another impostor does: It's called false freedom.

Perhaps you think you'd feel more freedom if there were fewer authorities over you telling you what to do, if you could just cater to your own needs and desires and not have to consider anybody else. You'd feel freer if there were fewer restrictions boxing you in. False freedom is ignoring authorities and breaking the rules.

False freedom is the goal of an 18-year-old Memphis man who ignored the law and robbed a convenience store for $235. An elderly diabetic didn't like his doctor's rule about no alcohol. A surgeon whose hobby was motorcycle riding didn't wear his helmet one afternoon even though his state's laws required a helmet. A middle-aged professor felt deadened by the principle of being faithful to his wife. A ten-year-old in San Francisco thought playing "hanging" would be fun, although his mother instructed him specifically not to play with ropes.

Ignoring authority, breaking a rule, is a statement of self: "I'm going to do what I want to do, and it feels wonderful."

When the pressure from restrictions and laws and rules and limitations builds, "busting out" is a natural response. You feel good and free — for a while.

But the 18-year-old who robbed the convenience store is locked up for 15 years in a Tennessee prison; the diabetic boozer is restricted to a hospital; the biker-surgeon is limited now by brain damage and a lost medical practice; the middle-aged professor is squeezed by huge alimony payments; and the disobedient ten-year-old died of hanging.

But the worst isn't going to happen to you, right? When you break the rules, you're careful. You watch the rear-view mirror constantly when you're speeding. You don't go to a legitimate tax-preparer, so if you fudge a bit, it'll never be reported. When you break sexual barriers for pleasure, you make sure you remain anonymous. You break restrictions of the confidences placed in you by gossiping only to non-mutual friends.

But is all this true freedom? When the restrictions are broken, your behavior appears free. But there's another term for it: license. It's what Christians fall into when they begin to say, "I don't bother to keep any commands; I'm free in Christ," or "There aren't any rules at all for Christians since we're free from the law," or "Breaking God's norms doesn't matter, because all my sins were forgiven on the cross; I can do whatever I want!" This is the freedom advocated by false religionists because it's so appealing to the strong desires of the old sin nature:

> For speaking out arrogant words of vanity, they entice by fleshly desires, by sensuality, those who barely escape from the ones who live in error, promising them freedom while they themselves are slaves of corruption; for by what a man is overcome, by this he is enslaved (2 Peter 2:18-19).

False freedom is either temporary, since it brings heavier restriction, or it's only external. Negating divine natural, social or personal laws isn't real freedom.

True Freedom

God says Christians are "called to freedom" (Galatians 5:1). It's not a freedom that avoids responsibility and "busts loose." Biblical freedom is a practical, positive stance filled with challenge. Let's think it through.

Every Christian is a possession of God. This may seem like a strange place to start, but visualize it: You're surrounded by God; He has you. The apostle Paul mentions that we're "people of God's own possession" (Titus 2:14; 1 Peter 2:9). The phrase is translated in the King James Version as "peculiar people." The Greek word for these phrases is a compound of "around" and the participial form of "to be" — "to be around." God completely surrounds you as a believer. Picture the concept as a dot — you — surrounded by a circle — God. Imagine anything — any incident, person, problem, any rule, law or restriction — having to be cleared by God before it ever reaches you. He's the one clearinghouse for your affairs; He's the one authority in your life. Any other sub-authority has to receive God's omniscient "okay" before laying any restriction on you. The principle is clear in passages such as Romans 13:1-7, where Paul says even pagan governments are to be obeyed because God can use them in your life as "ministers" of His authority. "There is no authority except from God, and those which exist are established by God" (Romans 13:1).

Man was designed to be subject to a stronger power. You can be a slave to sin (Romans 6:6), to the fear of death (Romans 8:15; Hebrews 2:15), to a condemning set of rules (Galatians 5:1), or a slave to God (Romans 6:22) and to righteousness (Romans 6:17). The benefits paid by sin as a master are "death" (Romans 6:21,23); but if you're "freed from sin and enslaved to God, you derive your benefit, resulting in sanctification, and the outcome eternal life" (Romans 6:22)

Believers are called "freedmen" (1 Corinthians 7:22). A freedman in the New Testament era was a slave who was sold to a god and couldn't be sold to another master. Paul calls himself a "bondslave" of Jesus Christ (Romans 1:1; Philippians 1:1; Titus 1:1). A bondslave was a family servant who chose to serve voluntarily in his master's household "because he loves . . . and fares well with" the master (Deuteronomy 15:12-17). The master would take the servant to the gates of the city — the "courtroom" of those days — and drive an awl through the servant's ear. The pierced ear would then be a sign that this servant served willingly; he loved his master.

God's respect for human choice is obvious in that His servants are voluntary freedmen and bondslaves, not lobotomized robots who have no choice but to serve Him. The picture of our relationship to God's authority gets even more dramatic when we realize that we freedmen and bondslaves are actually adopted as sons and daughters into God's household: "For you have not received a spirit of slavery leading to fear again, but . . . a spirit of adoption as sons by which we cry out, 'Abba! [Aramaic familiar term meaning "Daddy"] Father!' " (Romans 8:15; see also Galatians 4).

What master ultimately allows every order, rule, and restriction into your life? Well, that was pretty much of a Sunday School question, wasn't it? Even the back row sleepers could answer, "Jesus." But it's true; God is the one authority in your life. Peter and John proved the point when they had to tell their governing sub-authorities (who usually think they're sovereign authorities) that the only reason they obeyed the government was because a higher Authority told them to (Acts 4:18-20). When the sub-authorities ruled against the Authority, there was no contest as to whom the apostles would obey. God, who has you surrounded as His personal possession, is the one authority in your life. Everybody else is just acting on His authority, since all authority in heaven and earth has been given to Him (Matthew 28:18).

What's the point? One implication of your liberty is that you're "free from all men" (1 Corinthians 9:19). You don't have to be pulled apart trying to please everybody. The Bible reduces the number of authorities in your life to One.

As we've seen earlier, believers are free from their old natures — free from a legalistic framework of deadness that guarantees the only long-range result of all their best efforts will be deadness. Overlay that with an interesting comment by Liv Ullman in the preface to her book, *Choices:*

"I am learning that if I just go on accepting the framework for life that others have given me, if I fail to make my own choices, the reason for my life will be missing. I will be unable to recognize that which I have the power to change. I refuse to spend my life regretting the things I failed to do."[4]

We have choice as humans. We have the incredible choice of stepping out of our distorting, limiting sin natures — out of sin's dominion and the law's condemnation.

Knowing that we have freedom is only half the story. In the next chapter we'll look at the other half.

For Study, Thought and Discussion

Consider some of the restrictions and/or obligations that make you feel boxed in. The following statements and questions can be used as guidelines.

— Lack of money restricts my freedom. In what ways?

— I'm tied in a stifling relationship to a spouse, a child, my parents. Can the relationship be changed? Do I want it to change?

— My freedom is restricted by physical limitations. When does this bother me the most?

— I'm a slave to my temper. I'm a slave to (what other personality traits?) _____ .

— I'm bound to a ridiculous schedule. I can change that by (what means?) _____ .

— Religious rules keep me from doing what I want.

8

Liberty: Where the Spirit Is

Acting only according to your nature isn't real freedom. Any rhubarb plant or slug can act in a variety of ways according to their natures. Real human freedom isn't just having choices; it's having the power to choose and learning to choose rightly.

As Christians, it's OK to say that, at the time of my physical death, my old sin nature will no longer be a part of me (Romans 8:19-23). But it's good to be rid of its mastery over me in the here-and-now. If I remain bound in it, I'll never become all I can be — that is, who I want to be and who God designed me to be. An old-nature lifestyle is worthless if not destructive. I now need to learn to use my freedom. The apostle Peter writes, "Act as free men, and do not use your freedom as a covering for evil, but use it as bondslaves of God" (1 Peter 2:16). Liberated from their old selves, Christians are free to "no longer live for themselves, but for Him who died and rose again on their behalf"(2 Corinthians 5:15).

Freedom *From* Allows Freedom *To*

As we've seen, freedom is not just a lack of pressure, restriction and obligation. A comatose patient has no pressures, but certainly isn't free. Freedom means *ability:* If you're "free for dinner" you have no previous obligations and you're *able* to go out. A paraplegic is finally freed from the confines of a wheelchair and is able to walk with power provided by computerized electrical impulses activating nerve-dead muscles. A citizen in a free country is free from authoritarian manipulation and is able to work toward the lifestyle of his choosing.

I recently heard a karate expert describe freedom this way: One night, he was accosted by three knife-wielding toughs in an alley. As he assessed his attackers, he decided that not only could he hurt them, he also could outrun them. He finished the story by saying that, free from the threat of confrontation, he "laughed and freely ran with honor!"

Freedom *is* ability. It's the ability to say no to the demands of sin: to understand what it is in you that feels boxed-in by limitations; to adopt the values behind the norms and restrictions God allows in your life; to live in righteousness.

How can you have the abilities of freedom? Paul writes to the Corinthians, "Now the Lord is the Spirit; and where the Spirit of the Lord is, there is liberty" (2 Corinthians 3:17). Where is the Spirit of the Lord? If you're a believer, He's in your new nature — in you (Romans 8:9).

Once I choose to say no to the cravings and demands of my selfish old nature, the Spirit provides the ability to be free from sin's power. Have you had one or two areas of your life where you've been wrestling for a long, long time, areas where you've been losing the battle for freedom? When attacked by the full power of sin, I'm like the king whose first thought is surrender (Luke 14:31,32). I've learned that my own willpower doesn't match sin's power, and obeying sets of pious rules certainly has nothing to do with beating back sin. But the ability is His; the battle is His. My old nature "sets its desires against the Spirit, and the Spirit against the flesh; for these are in opposition to one another" (Galatians 5:17).

I, like Paul, have said, "Who will set me free from the body of this death? Thanks be to God through Jesus Christ our Lord!. . . For the law of the Spirit of life in Christ Jesus has set [me] free from the law of sin and of death" (Romans 7:24,25; 8:2). Freedom from sin's demands, freedom to overcome the distortions and limitations of the old sin nature is yours by choosing to submit to the Spirit. The ancient philosopher Seneca wisely held that "only as I bow to another authority am I free. Enslavement to myself is the worst bondage."

Freedom is the ability to understand your own God-given desires apart from the influence of your old nature. Bart often felt frustrated by the restriction that he couldn't just enjoy sex with anyone and everyone he met. He knew his God-given desires were fine, but he also knew that those desires often get warped by old-nature thoughts, attitudes and beliefs — such as Bart's familiar old tenet that women's bodies exist basically for male pleasure. Bart knew that the false freedom of breaking the restriction leads to worse restriction. He wanted to be authentically free from the frustration, the squeeze of the norm. So, after finding out God's truths on sex, his next step toward real sexual freedom was some Spirit-guided (James 1:5) soul-searching. What was his honest desire? He realized it by asking three "why's." Follow Bart through the process; then pick one of the rules you listed at the end of chapter 7, and ask yourself three times why you want to be free from that rule. Expect a tough time answering your third why.

Bart's first statement was, "I'd like to be free from the rule that I can't have sex with anyone I'd like."

Then he asked, "Why do I want freedom from that rule? Because I want more sexual, physical pleasure in my life.

"Why do I want more sexual, physical pleasure? Because I like it!

"Why do I like it so much? Because it's the only thing that seems to mean much to me now, that makes me feel life is exciting, the only thing that lets me feel completely satisfied. I want to do what my body tells me because physical pleasure is so much more real to me than any other pleasures."

Now it's your turn.

THE RULE:

Ask yourself:
Why do I want freedom from that rule?

Why?

Why?

What's the truth about what you really want? If you're honest, it will be your third answer. What does the Word say about that want?

Let's say Bart could experience what King David knew: "In Thy presence is fullness of joy; in Thy right hand there are pleasures forever" (Psalm 16:11), or "The children of men . . . drink their fill of the abundance of Thy house; and Thou dost give them to drink of the river of Thy delights. For with Thee is the fountain of life" (Psalm 36:8-9). If he felt genuinely satisfied with a life stuffed with other pleasures — meaningful activites, excitement, and delight every day at life's offerings (his real desire according to his third why) — would he feel cramped by the rule of not having casual sex with anyone and everyone? Probably not. The rule wouldn't matter. If *you* had what you really want, would the rules bother you? Probably not.

Generally, restrictions cramp our "surface" desires, the products of sin-warp on the deeper, truer desires of our hearts — the desires God promises to fulfill (Psalm 37:3-6). Remember that when you feel under bondage, it's usually your old sin nature that's squawking. You can break a rule for some false freedom that temporarily pacifies your old-nature-tainted surface desires. Or you can decide to handle the restriction — a choice that will move you closer to satisfying your true desires.

Understanding your own desires apart from old-nature-warping is important. But the primary step is to discover, understand as well as you can, and accept the values behind the restriction itself. Truth frees.

The process is familiar to most of us. Let's say a restricting norm, a pressurizing schedule, and an irritating person all waltz into your life at once. The truth to adopt as a solid base of your freedom is that, since God is the one authority in your life, all the responsibilities, obligations, rules, orders, laws and limitations that hit you are allowed by Him (though not necessarily initiated by Him). He won't let any more hit you than you can handle, of course (1 Corinthians 10:13). He "works all these things together for good" for you (Romans 8:28). The pressure gets your attention so God can put His process to work toward completing you, conforming you to His image (James 1:2-4). The more a rule squeezes, the more you know it represents a value area God wants you to understand, an area in which He wants you to feel free.

It is vital that you allow God's Spirit to guide you into the Word to find the truth about this situation — about the value of the restricting rule, about how to prioritize schedule demands, about why and how to love an irritating person. As you decide to adopt God's thoughts on the subject — which is a step of faith — the Spirit uses this renewed thought to transform you just one more degree to be more like Christ. And Christ always feels free. In your new step of Christlikeness, you understand the situation and have the ability to handle it, to live through it as if it's no restriction at all — as if the pressure is "pure joy"! (James 1:2) It's the freedom of an old Bob Dylan song: "How good does it feel to be free?. . . How free are the birds in the chains of the skyways?" The non-sin-warped, true desires of your heart — which nicely bubble to the surface as you're transformed to Christlikeness — are actually fulfilled, not restricted by God's "restrictions."

How this process works warrants a closer look. As a disciple — a follower-learner — of Christ, the Spirit of truth "will guide you into all the truth" (John 16:13). "If you abide in (His) Word... you shall know the truth, and the truth shall make you free" (John 8:31-32). The word "know" in the original Greek is *ginosko,* meaning more than just taking in information on a brain level; it means to understand or to understand completely. In the phrase "those who believe and *know* the truth" (1 Timothy 4:3), the word *epiginosko* suggests an even deeper involvement in knowing the truth. "To know" in this verse means "to observe, fully perceive, notice attentively, discern, to participate in the truth," according to *Vine's Expository Dictionary of New Testament Words.* When you know as an integrated value in your soul the truth about your desires and God's values, the knowledge allows you to act in Spirit-guided righteousness against which "there is no law" or restriction (Galatians 5:23).

Some incidental fine print: Knowing the truth doesn't always mean you'll understand God's exact rationale for a restriction on you. God doesn't expect us to understand truth we can't handle, and you shouldn't either. Faith is not rationally understanding the fine-tunings of the universe. Faith is trusting the truth He has revealed; knowing His revealed truth makes us free.

As a three-year-old reaches toward a stove, his parents shout, "Don't touch that burner!" He feels this is an authoritarian, arbitrary restriction. When he comes to understand the value behind the restriction — preferably not learning it the hard way — he agrees that not touching the burner is a good rule to observe. When, as an eleven-year-old, the same child walks through the kitchen and glances at the red-hot burner, does he feel restricted by an authoritarian, arbitrary rule? Or does he observe the rule because he, too, believes it is true? Having adopted his parent's perspective on the danger of touching burners, he's so free in handling the rule that he doesn't even think about it as a rule; not frying his fingers is simply part of him.

You're free to do what's right. Yes, Christian freedom is positional; but it's also practical. According to the Word, anyone consistently walking in the Spirit will act right from right motives like "love, joy, peace, patience, kindness, goodness, faithfulness, gentleness, self-control" (Galatians 5:22-23). Again, nothing squeezes actions prompted by these qualities — "against such things there is no law" (Galatians 5:23). Freedom is the ability to handle restrictions because you're living these qualities.

Besides establishing the idea that we have choice, how does freedom-as-new-nature-ability tie in with our study on ethics? You see, on a human level, the reason we had a few anxious/critical/flustered feelings as we studied through those chapters on laws is that doing right and not doing wrong cramps humans' style. Ethics doesn't feel like fun. Face it: Every right or wrong ordered by God is a restriction, an obligation, a limit, a rule to an old-nature-enslaved person. That's why non-Christians can mimic Christian ethics, but can't feel free in them.

But you can feel free even while living an ethical lifestyle. Think of it: you can maintain your integrity, develop a rich character, be a good person and at the same time feel happy about it, with your deepest desires unrestricted. Area by area, restriction by restriction, you can choose freedom from sin-nature limitations, freedom to know and grow into truth — to handle the norms of righteousness.

Your Spirit-guided knowledge of the truth gives you the privilege of discerning God's rights and wrongs for your life in those fuzzy, gray areas — the activities, the attitudes, the possibilities about which the Bible has no explicit commands. Each absolute value or principle of Scripture is a truth; each truth has myriad applications. And God leaves it to believers to "become accustomed to the word of righteousness," to think so much the way God thinks that "because of practice [they] have their senses trained to discern good and evil" (Hebrews 5:13-14), even in the fuzzy ethical quandaries of life. I'm free to be guided by God's Spirit and, applying the truths of the general principles of the Word, to develop my own personal, specific applications as my own personal rights and wrongs.

Here, of course, is where professional legalists are threatened; they "sneak in to spy out our liberty which we have in Jesus Christ, in order to bring us into bondage" (Galatians 2:4). They feel it's dangerous for Christians to act as individual priests before God.

But it's not that God "forgot" to give us every specific application of His values; He purposely left them in generalities just so we'd have to struggle through their application. It's the throwing of ourselves on Him, the Spirit-guided struggling to discern life-and-death applications of good and evil that grows us. So legalistic fears notwithstanding, believers are free to personally apply God's norms.

In the helter-skelter of new ethical questions, this phase of our liberty is so critical that we'll devote the last third of our study to it. We'll get good at submitting to the Spirit, understanding the truths of several scriptural principles, and applying those principles to sticky, puzzling gray areas. And the conclusions you'll come up with will be authoritative in the context of your life, because you're free to know and to live God's specific direction of what's right and what isn't for you — free to live the best possible life.

Be Free

Imagine that you face a right/wrong decision, and you determine to act in the character of Christ. Did He feel boxed-in, pressured, irritated, obligated, restricted by acting righteously? Neither will you as you're transformed to become like Him: Though a slave of sin, "you became obedient from the heart to that form of teaching to which you were committed, and, having been freed from sin, you became a slave to righteousness" (Romans 6:17-18).

Feel free:
— free from domination by any authority other than God Himself;
— free from the hypocritical hassle of maintaining a proper Christian image;
— free from the power of sin;
— free from your thoughts and feelings always being tainted by sin;

— free to say no to worthless or destructive actions, thoughts, attitudes;

— free to sense freedom in the middle of pressure;

— free to understand universal truths;

— free to live God's style of life.

For Study, Thought and Discussion

Identifying root causes in our lives is tough. How does this section relate to life-controlling attitudes and sins?

Re-read the discussion with Bart and your responses in this chapter on pages 92-93. Call to mind another rule you would like to be free from. Again ask yourself three times, "Why do I want to be free from that rule?" Take special note of the answer to your third why.

9
The Synthesis

Christian ethics is a synthesized trinity of law, love and liberty.

Most of us crew members on the Gulf of Mexico drilling rig called him Kojak; a few of the roughnecks called him "chrome dome." He'd lost his hair during the Battle of the Bulge, according to one of his yarns. Now, as galley hand and chief teller of tales aboard our offshore platform, Kojak patted and polished his head as if it were his medal of valor; it was his only medal.

One balmy night in April, he and I sat out on the rear deck while the water sparkled phosphorescent around the shrimpers plying the gulf around us.

"You wormy roughnecks figure you got it all ahead of you," he began; and I knew I was in for another sad, ain't-life-miserable story from the old guy.

He patted his head: "I done it all wrong. All wrong. Ever tell you about the girl I had in Memphis? She was a pretty one. Give me a son. He's out there somewheres now." He waved toward the north, and I couldn't look at his watery eyes as he began cataloging all the misadventures, the heartbreaks, the dreams he figured he'd lost in a brown paper bag somewhere in a bus station. Finally he grunted up from the bench and said, "I tried to do what was right. So how come it didn't work?"

I didn't say anything. There's no easy answer to the cruelty and complexity a slapdash ethical system can wreak over a lifetime of sincerely trying to do what's right. I guess I could have said something about life being something we do, and like everything else we do, life is stuffed with how-to's. Whether you're going to be a pinball wizard, integrate your business files, have tea with a Tibetan lama, or go juggin' for catfish, there are ways to do it and ways not to.

Right Living Has Some Basic Requirements

We've covered the basics of God's system of ethics in the last several chapters but let's review for clarity.

A classic statement of Christ's call is, "If anyone wishes to come after Me, let him deny himself, and take up his cross daily, and follow Me" (Luke 9:23). Regardless of all the fragmented workshops, books, sermons and lessons on the pieces and compartmentalized topics of Christianity, the real thing always boils down to the gestalt, the unified wholeness, of God living in humans. But we seem to need to be scientific, to break things down into their component parts to understand them.

So let's boil every description of Christianity down to the three basics: law, love and liberty. The three phases of responding to Christ's call involve (1) denying self in salvation and sanctification, (2) taking up our cross daily in Spirit-control, and (3) following His direction in the Word.

Denying your old self is critical to a working ethical system. God's laws condemn the old, human nature, since God insists His norms are to be observed, and since old-nature-bound humans can't observe them all. Saying no to your old self in salvation ensures that you won't be condemned by the *law,* that you're out from under the curse of the law because you've been declared righteous in salvation.

God's *love* is poured out in your heart (Romans 5:5) that first time you deny your old self, and you're finally able to act in selfless agape-style love. Saying no to your old self in service to God and others ensures you'll want to do right things.

God's *liberty* frees you from sin's mastery when you first deny your old self in salvation. You can freely choose — without the control of sin tainting your every decision — the right.

Living in the new life of the Spirit is another requisite to the best possible life. Taking up your cross daily signifies not only death to your old self but daily commitment to new life in the Spirit. The requirements of God's *laws* are fulfilled in us — not by us (Romans 8:4) — as we yield to the control of His Spirit within us.

Love, the substance of moral living, is an automatic result or "fruit" of the Holy Spirit's direction of our lives (Galatians 5:22).

Liberty is "where the Spirit of the Lord is" (2 Corinthians 3:17) because it is by His power that we have the ability to handle the restrictions of God's norms.

Following Christ as He is revealed in the Word is another key to living out righteousness. The Word embodies the *"law* of Christ" (Galatians 6:2,13) and illustrates how we're to "follow in His steps" (1 Peter 2:21).

Love is following the commands of God's Word in attitude and action in all three areas of relationship: with God, others and self.

Liberty is offered to those who "abide in [His] Word," because they'll then know the truth and "the truth shall make [them] free" (John 8:31,32).

The synthesis is obvious. Denying the old self, taking up the standard of new life in the Spirit, and following Christ as revealed in the Word — salvation, Spirit-control, and saturation in the Book — are the keys to understanding and living out God's laws, love and liberty.

Putting It Together

Law, love and liberty are, in turn, only ingredients in the solid synthesis of God's system of ethics. God's norms define the parameters of right and wrong; God's love is the essence of living the right and rejecting the wrong; and God's liberty is the milieu in which it's possible for a human to choose righteousness. When each element of the synthesis is genuine and balanced, life is lived as it was designed. For instance, notice the interaction of liberty, love, and law in Paul's statement to the Galatians:

> For you were called to freedom, brethren; only do not turn your freedom into an opportunity for the flesh, but through love serve one another. For the whole law is fulfilled in one word, in the statement, "You shall love your neighbor as yourself" (Galatians 5:13-14).

Law, love and liberty are inherently interactive be-

cause they're perspectives of the same essential righteousness of God. Living out the synthesis, as James
Packer sees it in his essay, "Conscience, Choice and
Character," is "practical moral reason, consciously exercised, growing in insight and sureness of guidance
through instruction and use, and bringing inner inte-
gration, health and peace to those who obey it."[1]

The biblical idea of ethics starts with the nature of
God and how that nature, growing in the soul of a
human being (2 Peter 1:4), manifests divine inner qualities in actions "against which there is no law" (Galatians 5:23, KJV).The biblical pattern of ethics isn't utilita-
rian, although it does "work." It's not intuitional, although it "clicks" with the gut-level feelings of the
believer who wants to do what's right. And it isn't
rationalistic, although it does make sense. Most of the
dozens of varieties and labels of ethical systems —
which usually have just enough truth to be dangerous
— are simply fragments of the true, synthesized ethics
of God.

Pharisees seem to start with the external norms of
life, and then gauge how someone like you, or someone
like Jesus Christ, fulfills those laws. The Greeks of
New Testament times and their counterparts today
focus on internal human qualities such as love, and,
as if the qualities have lives of their own, those people
enjoy the experiments of watching how these qualities
act.

But ethics has to be seen as a synthesis, since righteousness is an expression of God's character; and He's
obviously synthesized. We should be holy — because
there are rules about holiness? — because it's the loving
thing to do? — because we can? No: "You shall be
holy, for I am holy" (1 Peter 1:16). We can "put on
the new self, which in the likeness of God has been
created in righteousness and holiness of the truth"
(Ephesians 4:24). Face it, even highly ethical humans

with the decision-making help of computerized artificial intelligence can't live best-possible, righteous lives without Him.

Conscience

We can see how this synthesized system should work by taking a quick look at the basic human ethical barometer: your conscience.

Let's say you've just slid into your usual booth at the Hog's Breath Eatery, ready to drown your gloom in a French Chocolate Almond milkshake, because you just received a car insurance premium notice for $350 — money that you were going to spend on new stereo speakers. There on the seat next to you is a beat-up purse, with no identification cards, just a wad of bills wrapped in a rubber band. Your eyes get bigger and bigger as you count out almost $400 in cash!

Your conscience, meanwhile, begins involuntarily pronouncing all the things you believe you should do about finding someone else's valuables. Your honesty and integrity tell you that you have no right to things that don't belong to you — that is not loving your neighbor, whoever she may be.

And that last part catches you. Exactly who is this neighbor? What if she's some wealthy eccentric who doesn't need the money anyway? What if you turn the purse in to the store manager and it conveniently "disappears" before the owner returns to claim it — if she ever does?

Decisions, decisions.

You can readily see that conscience is not necessarily automatic; it involves reason and will. It describes the internal mechanism of choosing right over wrong. God promises that "the blood of Christ . . . [will] cleanse your conscience from dead works to serve the living

God" (Hebrews 9:14). But since conscience resides in the soul, it can be controlled by either your Spirit-filled new nature or your dead-works-filled old nature. So a solid Christian ethic can't be a simplistic adage of "Let your conscience be your guide."

Thomas Aquinas described the conscience as having *synderesis* and *conscientia,* the abilities to *see* moral truths and to *apply* them. Later ethicists followed Aquinas's breakdown, explaining that the conscience somehow handles ethical theory and practice. For our purposes, let's accept the definition as the conscience mechanism that rests in our craniums.

Back to your purse-finding incident. Your thoughts rest upon a basic, major premise — a premise you honestly believe true: I have no right to things that don't belong to me. The next step is to align with or violate your major premise: I now have a lost purse which doesn't belong to me. What if I hang on to the purse? What if I hand it over? The conclusion comes next: I have no right to whatever is in this purse, so I should take the purse to the counter and tell the manager that I found it in booth number 7. Conscience in action is major premise, minor premise, conclusion. Good feelings often come when you act according to the conclusion; guilt feelings often come when you act otherwise.

The more carefully you analyze the facts of minor-premise situations, the wiser you'll be in judging whether a minor premise aligns with or violates a major premise. And so your conclusions will be more accurate.

Incidentally, the conscience of the Bible is not what Freud associated with conscience; his "super-ego" was not biblical conscience but false guilt. Neuroses, which feed on false guilt, thrive in a person whose major premises are faulty, who has false beliefs about what's true. Further faulty judgment is a problem in a person who will not or simply does not examine the actual or projected situations that constitute minor premises. A "seared," cauterized, insensitive conscience results from ignoring true conclusions.

What happens when somebody like my old buddy, Kojak, tackles life with the aid of his conscience — but without salvation, the Spirit or the Word? His major premises may be faulty since he doesn't consider God's truths. Many people's major premises are nothing but hearsay or old adages (better safe than sorry; never trust anybody with a cheap cigar; women were made to keep house and make babies), or authoritarian voices from the past (Shirley, if there's one thing you must never do in life, it's never, never marry a preacher), or any number of manmade attempts at truth. Manmade truths, even when mixed in with actual truth, lead only toward faulty judgment, false conclusions, mistakes, sin and guilt, no matter how sincere the attempt.

So conscience, enslaved and blinded by the old-nature principle of sin, is a poor device for determining what's best and what isn't. But let's hang onto the mechanism of conscience as a good model for how believers can process rights and wrongs, because consciences can be transformed as minds are transformed by knowledge of the truth (1 Corinthians 8:1-8).

But it's being a growth process doesn't mean it isn't practical. Getting into physical shape is a discouragingly long haul for many people, but the process still is segmented into daily steps of progress — 20 more situps, another hour of aerobics, 500 less calories. Living out righteousness happens one truth at a time, one area, one habit, one determination, one degree to another of becoming like Christ. Your conscience operates in your soul. Under the tutelage of the Spirit, it sits down at the console of your computer-brain and calls up the file regarding a right and wrong situation you're facing. The screen pops with reactions, thoughts, attitudes, beliefs, old scenes which you'd keyed in under the tutelage of your old master sin. The Spirit directs you through the software manual to delete, merge, insert, erase completely, and to key in true data. You decide to follow each of the Spirit's directions, then to save the renewed file as a microdot on your brain's memory. You're transformed, one thought at a time.

Even on a thoroughly human level, conscience and moral thinking develops in stages. Lawrence Kohlberg of the School of Education at Harvard has augmented earlier work by Jean Piaget on the typical developmental stages of morals. In the pre-moral level, Stage Zero reflects a childish mindset that good is what is pleasant and bad is what is not. In Kohlberg's preconventional level, Stage One development is characterized by the person choosing right or wrong according to reward or punishment. A Stage Three moralist is guided by personal satisfaction and to some extent the satisfaction of others; it's the "Be-good-to-me-and-I'll-be-good-to-you" stage. The conventional level of Kohlberg's model suggests a Stage Three person will be guided by the approval and expectations of others. There is also a Stage Four person, who understands the need for rules and authority, and so does the right thing out of respect for authority, duty and social order.

The next level is the principled level, in which a person tries to find values that are true in their own right apart from the coercion or approval of a social group. Stage Five moralists believe that the purpose of laws in society is to preserve human rights. Although they tend to adopt standards of their social group, they're open to change according to values. Stage Six is Kohlberg's highest category. Here morality isn't founded in legality or specific rules but in abstract principles; Stage Six standards are individual matters of conscience.

Although Kohlberg's stages are keyed to social morality, the pattern is interesting as it applies to personal rights and wrongs. Ruth Beechick observed, "Although the United States Constitution is based on stage five, most adult Americans are at stages three and four. The emphasis of our society is on being a good neighbor and obeying the laws of the land. Those who operate either lower or higher than convention dictates may pay the penalty. But unlike the stage-two person who dislikes the law because it interferes with his personal freedom and selfish demands, the stage-five or stage-six person, having progressed through stages three and four, understands the reason for the law and respects it. . . The moral-judgment approach (of stage six) recognizes that true morality comes from within the individual rather than being imposed upon him."[2]

Christian ethics is definitely Stage Six material. As you dig deeper into the solid "word of righteousness," you'll become one of those "who because of practice have their senses trained to discern good and evil" (Hebrews 5:13-14). As the God of love helps you "abound still more and more in real knowledge and all discernment," you'll be able to "approve the things that are excellent" (Philippians 1:9-10). You'll be "one who looks intently at the perfect law, the law of liberty, and abides by it" (James 1:25). A saved, Spirit-controlled, Word-saturated Christian who enjoys the synthesis of law and love and liberty can know and live out what's right.

Choices

That we may "choose what is best" (Philippians 1:10 GNB) suggests a Spirit-guided style of deliberating. Of thinking.

My sluggish mind would much rather fall for the "I'm-an-empty-headed-vessel-so-nudge-me-sweet-Jesus" school of religious ethics. That way, if things don't turn out well, I can always secretly blame Him.

But, unless God chooses to miraculously make stones cry out or have unskilled, ignorant-of-His-Word, unthinking minds accomplish amazing feats, the Spirit uses what He finds in us. Gazing into the Word puts truth at the Spirit's disposal to use in His transformation process. His sanctification isn't by osmosis or by wishful thinking. It's by faith (2 Thessalonians 2:13), by our deciding to trust what we find in God's Word.

But this God-given responsibility to think and choose is an uphill battle for several reasons.

First, we're firmly ensconced in an age that insists there are no black-and-white absolutes. "Everything's relative" has grown like crabgrass from a philosophical speculation to a reason not to look for what's true. Although it's black-and-white true or false that you are now playing a tuba, we still tend to slur "Everything's relative" to all of life, as if it's impossible to determine whether an action does or does not violate a divine norm, as if it's impossible that the divine norm itself is true or false. Just because much of life is not black or white (mince pie can be so-so or great or abominable; people are neither wholly humanly good nor bad; fault in divorce cases rarely belongs to one party). But everything is not muddled in gray relativity. In your Spirit-guided thinking, you'll often find that the notorious gray areas of ethics are only, in the context of your own life, intricate variations of blacks and whites.

Second, we're mechanistic. Since Sir Francis Bacon's Novum Organum in the early 1600's, we've competently trained ourselves to think left-brain scientifically — to trust only what can be verified and cross-verified by human senses and, better yet, by instrumentation. So we're nearly hopeless utilitarians: If we've proved a theorem by seeing that it works, it's proven and, only then, true. We therefore tend to mistrust an idea that can't be quantified and empirically proven, such as the mystical synthesis of law, love and liberty.

Third, we don't like rules. Especially ones that cramp our style, or ones we don't understand. For instance, God's norms on marriage as a lifelong monogamous relationship are usually branded as outdated. But I think the West hasn't toyed long enough with the alternatives to agree with God. Yet.

Fourth, we're in a Christian culture of magical realists. Magical Realism is practiced by a school of predominantly South American writers whose stories are mostly realistic yet which include jarring elements of the fantastic. For example, an ordinary circus performer and his son happen to discover diamonds in ordinary oranges — just as many Christians think of their lives as ordinary and real, with the aberrative presence of God as only a small, magical spark that makes life "nice."

Fifth, we're not used to thinking. Most of us have fallen into ambitious, or respectable, or just plain frantic schedules that have virtually left us no time to think about anything beyond personal problems and escapist fantasy. How would your maturity be affected if you, as many of our great-grandparents did, spent nearly every evening thinking? Imagine the hours of staring into the fire, the books you'd read, the winter days of thinking long, long thoughts. (Sound strangely like the vacation your soul and body seem to crave?) No, I don't think our ancestors were more educated or smarter than we are. But I do think they were deeper people; the life-texture of today's One-Minute-Thinker is ultimately sawdust.

So plan to challenge yourself to thinking, deliberating, choosing. As only C. S. Lewis could put it, your right and wrong choosing is at the core of who you become:

Every time you make a choice you are turning the central part of you, the part of you that chooses, into something a little different from what it was before. And taking your life as a whole, with all your innumerable choices, all your life long you are slowly turning this central thing either into a heavenly creature or into a hellish creature; either into a creature that is in harmony with God, and with other creatures, and with itself, or else into one that is in a state of war and hatred with God, and with its fellow-creatures, and with itself.[3]

For Study, Thought and Discussion

How can we know right from wrong? Work through these steps:
- Get straight with God. Make sure that you have put your trust in God and that you are controlled by the Holy Spirit (Ephesians 5:18 and 1 John 1:9).
- Study the truth. Pray for guidance to know the truth (John 16:13) as you study the Word on an ethical quandary. Your major premise is to be the truth about that topic as expressed in God's values, principles and commands.

Discuss personal, ethical dilemmas with a Christian friend or a study group. Pray for wisdom (James 1:5) as you biblically or extra-biblically research the facts of the situation surrounding the quandary — giving you an accurate minor premise. Does or will the situation align with or violate the truth? Is a higher-valued norm potentially violated?

Decide. Whose values will you live by?

Sound too simplistic? Not when you consider the meaning of each of those steps. If it seems too simple, however, isn't that exactly what you'd expect when every human regardless of intellect has to determine rights and wrongs?

Undoubtedly you've got some good questions on the validity or rationale of this simple system. But I think the best way to crystallize those questions and to work through answers is by putting the pattern to work. Let's get practical.

10
When Righteousness Gets Personal

Loving yourself properly — body, soul and spirit — isn't as easy as it sounds. Sometimes our inner and outer selves are like two different people. The disparity between who we are and who we want to be can be painful. But God wants to ease that pain and guide us to wholeness.

Much of that wholeness comes with a clear conscience about loving your body-soul-spirit self properly; so many of the basic principles of Scripture focus on setting norms that directly affect only you. (Indirect effects, of course, eventually ripple into your relationships with others and with God.) So if there's a good place to start putting together an ethical lifestyle, it's where you live — in your self.

Before looking at any particular principles, review some biblical foundations of your value to God. Remember the hierarchical scale of values that dictate exemptions when norms conflict? You're right up there close to God — you were created in His image (Genesis

1:26,27), which means, among other things, that you
were designed to be like God in knowledge, righteousness and holiness of the truth (Ephesians 4:24; Colossians 3:10). You're going to exist forever (1 Corinthians
15:53). You were carefully designed as a unique, wonderful person (Psalm 139:13-16), and you're God's idea
of a masterpiece (literal translation of "We are His
workmanship," Ephesians 2:10).

God knows you intimately (Psalm 139:1-5; Matthew
10:30). The importance of your life is recorded in heav-
en — from your name (Luke 10:20; Revelations 13:8;
21:27) to the length of your days (Psalm 139:16). And
He still loves you (1 John 4:10)!

God says that you are somebody. Although the
world-system frantically insists otherwise, you're valuable, not because of what you have or do — not because
of your appearance (1 Samuel 16:7), physical abilities
(Psalm 147:10-11), intelligence (1 Corinthians 1:26-27),
possessions (Luke 12:15 — since everything belongs to
God — 1 Chronicles 29:11), or accomplishments (Isaiah
64:6, John 15:5, Acts 17:25-28). You're valuable because
God made you. And you know the saying: "God don't
make no junk."

You can look on that biblical portrait of yourself as
just so much self-help-hype. Or you can look at it as
the truth: God says you're infinitely valuable. Do you
trust what God says about you in these verses, or are
you like the clay arguing with the potter about what
he's made (Isaiah 45:9, Romans 9:20)? Whose standards
of your value are you going to believe — yours, Charles
Darwin's, Madison Avenue's, or God's?

Maybe all this talk of self sounds unspiritual and
selfish. Of course, that depends on which self you're
talking about. Use discernment as you consider hating
your old self but loving your new self — the new
nature controlling your body, soul and spirit. Old-self
thinking *is* selfish: You're to "lay aside the old self with

its evil practices" (Colossians 3:9). But thinking straight about your self is commanded (Romans 12:3); you're to "love your neighbor as you love yourself" (Luke 10:27). How do you properly love yourself? "And this is love, that we walk according to His commandments" (2 John 6); that is, you love yourself properly by taking on God's standards of your self-identity and self-worth.

No doubt about it: You'll need to be comfortable in thinking what God thinks about you before these right-and-wrong deliberations about yourself will "work."

Weight

Imagine the colosseum, the grandstand crowd, the well-marked cinder track and the taut muscles of a sprinter kneeling into the starting blocks. The apostle Paul equates the Christian life to a race (1 Corinthians 9:24-27) in which every believer is hot-footing it toward the finish line of becoming like Christ (Romans 8:29). Contemporary Christian singer Twila Paris sings, "Runner, though the race is long, feel like giving in, but you're holding on; runner, when the race is won, you will run into His arms."[1] The allusion, of course, is to Hebrews 12:1: "Therefore, since we have so great a cloud of witnesses surrounding us, let us also lay aside every encumbrance, and the sin which so easily entangles us, and let us run with endurance the race that is set before us, fixing our eyes on Jesus. . . ."

Running with a buddy on my back was part of Army bootcamp training. But when the point isn't training any more, when the running is serious, excess weight is out. When I enter a race, even in nasty weather, I don't put on anything that'll slow me down and make the race harder. When a soldier enters actual combat, running with an extra 180 pounds on his back is suicide.

If you're a believer, you are in the race. And it's serious; it's your life. You don't need and eventually will regret anything that makes it harder to run, any weight that slows you down from becoming more like Jesus Christ. (See 1 Corinthians 9:24-27; see Matthew 19:16-24 as an example of excess.)

Profitability

"All things are lawful for me," the free-thinking apostle Paul wrote. "But not all things are profitable" (1 Corinthians 6:12b).

I was a boob-tube addict as a kid. I watched hundreds of hours of crackly old "Little Rascals" episodes and "Leave It To Beaver" and "I Love Lucy." My eyes were chronically bloodshot and my skin a lovely shade of television-gray. But as every tube addict must eventually realize, TV was mostly a wonderful time-waster. Most of my viewing-time was spent hoping that something really captivating would come on next, so I'd hang on for another program, flipping through the channels with something of an ache for excitement or laughs. Much as I hated to admit it, those daily hours of canned laughter and faked punches could easily have been spent doing something that would have challenged me more, taught me more about real life. It hit me in high school that, often for months at a time, the most interesting things in my life were television shows!

Are you much of a chess player? If you're on my level, I sit down to a match and figure, move-by-move what could happen if I moved here or here. A master chess player, they say, sees the pattern of a game and doesn't worry about step-by-step moves. He simply rejects the moves that don't fit. Is there any rational reason to make a move opposite to the direction of your game's finish? To program your mind with value-decisions opposite to whom you're becoming (see Philippians 4:8)?

That's the principle of profitability: even innocent moves that don't fit into God's plan for you aren't part of your best possible life.

Control

"All things are lawful for me, but I will not be mastered by anything" (1 Corinthians 6:12b). If something or someone will enslave me, giving me no choice (although I technically always have a choice) but to jump back under my old sin nature, it violates the control principle. If I surrender the Spirit-control of my heart-mind to it, it's wrong.

An explicit norm reflecting this principle is: "Do not get drunk with wine, for that is dissipation" (Ephesians 5:18). A drunk gives up control of his body, soul and spirit to wine, which is "dissipation," or a definite waste.

What's the point? Matching a questioned activity against a brain-level principle isn't all there is to determining your personal rights and wrongs. For instance: Find someone who knows computer programming; have that person list all the norms of Scripture and set up a program whereby you could ask, Does this activity/choice violate any scriptural norms? You will get an answer in a millisecond. Would you have a system of biblical ethics? No, you would have electronic legalism.

God isn't interested in one-shot decisions to align with a biblical norm; that sort of "righteousness" goes right back to the futility of God's people giving Him lip-service, sacrifices and external piety even when their hearts are far from Him. Instead, get used to doing some hefty, Spirit-guided Bible study. The more important the subject, the more study you'll have to tackle. It's in the Spirit-led saturation of the truth that

God changes your values to His; then you can know
and do exactly what God wants.

Bodily Care

It may be bulging in the mezzanine, but "your body
is a temple of the Holy Spirit who is in you, whom
you have from God, and . . . you are not your own.
For you have been bought with a price: therefore glorify
God in your body" (1 Corinthians 6:19,20 italics added).

Your body and everything in it is God's. So it's reasonable that you actualize Paul's injunction "to present
your bodies a living and holy sacrifice, acceptable to
God, which is your spiritual service of worship" (Romans 12:1). Although God owns your body, your old
nature can easily pretend ownership and use your
arms, voice, brain, eyes, etc., as "instruments of unrighteousness" (see Romans 6:6,12-13). Or you can
choose to yield the use of your body with *all* its parts
to God for His use.

Don't minimize your body because it's only physical.
Religious sects throughout history have made the mistake of branding the body as evil. A little Spirit-guided,
Bible-digging will reveal that God values your body —
so much so that He planned for you to be trustworthy
in the stewardship of your body (1 Corinthians 4:2).

Be sure to think through this "body principle" as it
relates to sexuality. Consider this surprising statement:
"Every other sin that a [person] commits is outside
the body, but the immoral [person] sins against his
own body" (1 Corinthians 6:18). Think also through
the interrelation of the "body" and "control" principles
as old-sin-nature-warped sexual desires try to control
your body (Romans 1:26-27; 1 Corinthians 6:9-11; 7:2-5;
1 Thessalonians 4:3-8).

Conscience

We've dealt with the general machinations of conscience, but we also need to realize that God imposes as a norm the principle of maintaining a clear conscience (see Acts 24:16, 2 Corinthians 1:12, 1 Timothy 1:5). Even a believer who is "weak in the faith" (Romans 14:1), who is "not accustomed to the word of righteousness" (Hebrews 5:13), is to maintain a clear conscience in the "gray areas" of right and wrong.

Two gray areas — activities about which there are no explicit commands — in Paul's time were the observance of religious holidays and the eating of meat which had been offered to idols, and which was therefore sold at bargain prices! Paul writes,

> One man regards one day above another, another regards every day alike. Let each man be fully convinced in his own mind. . . . I know and am convinced in the Lord Jesus that nothing is unclean in itself; but to him who thinks anything to be unclean, to him it is unclean. . . . (Romans 14:5,14).

In the case of eating meat once offered to idols, some Christians couldn't shake the major premise that the idols they had earlier worshipped actually had mystical power. Elsewhere, Paul writes,

> We know that there is no such thing as an idol in the world, and that there is no God but one. . . . However not all men have this knowledge; but some, being accustomed to the idol until now, eat food as if it were sacrificed to an idol; and their conscience being weak is defiled   (1 Corinthians 8:4,7).

Notice in Romans the clarity of the principle as it relates to a person's knowledge of what God has said:

> The faith which you have, have as your own
> conviction before God. Happy is he who does
> not condemn himself in what he approves. But
> he who doubts is condemned if he eats [meat
> offered to idols], because his eating is not from
> faith; and whatever is not from faith is sin (Ro-
> mans 14:22,23).

The obvious exhortation here is growth in faith, finding out the truth of what God says and deciding to trust it. But in the meantime, if a believer isn't sure what God says about an activity, or, because of past experiences, can't shake a false major premise, God's principle is: Maintain a clear conscience. Paul fiercely protects the integrity of those who lack knowledge or haven't lost past associations; he asserts their right to conclude that a certain activity is wrong for them even though other believers seem to find it an innocent expression of their freedom (Romans 14). Yet he still encourages the strong to help the weak toward understanding the major premises of God's truths (Romans 15:1-2). In the meantime, his advice is almost tongue-in-cheek practical: "Eat anything that is sold in the meat market, without asking questions for conscience' sake; for the earth is the Lord's, and all it contains" (1 Corinthians 10:25).

The use of this principle for our transformation to Christlikeness is pretty simple: Don't violate your Spirit-controlled conscience. The implications of the principle are profound: The same activity can be solidly, biblically sinful to one believer and solidly, biblically clean for another. We're not to force our convictions regarding gray areas onto others.

For Study, Thought and Discussion

Check under True (+) or False (−) as you answer the principles' statements. If your questioned activity just doesn't seem to apply, or if you cannot determine a definite true or false, leave that particular response blank.

If a minus appears, you know that God is saying to you personally that this activity isn't the best way for you to live. It would violate a scriptural principle in your case; it would be wrong. If only a string of plus marks result, there's a healthy chance that this activity is right for you.

These obviously aren't all the principles in the Word; five is a pretty slim representation of the principles covering the "gray areas" of living. So don't presume that the results of this checklist will be the final say on everything.

Now, using the wisdom of the Spirit, work through some or all of the following questions, guided by the chart below.

1. Is my drinking alcohol right or wrong?

Reference	Principle	True	False
Weight:			
Hebrews 12:1	It doesn't slow me down spiritually.	___	___
Profitability:			
1 Cor. 6:12a	It can be profitable, useful.	___	___
Control:			
1 Cor. 6:12b	I can be Spirit-controlled in this.	___	___
Bodily Care:			
1 Cor. 6:19,20	This represents good stewardship of my body.	___	___
Conscience:			
Romans 14:5	My sanctified conscience can be clear.	___	___

Therefore, at least at this stage, this activity is: _____ right wrong _____ for me.

2. If I find $50 on the street, is it right to keep it?

Reference	Principle	True	False
Weight:			
Hebrews 12:1	It doesn't slow me down spiritually.	_____	_____
Profitability:			
1 Cor. 6:12a	It can be profitable, useful.	_____	_____
Control:			
1 Cor. 6:12b	I can be Spirit-controlled in this.	_____	_____
Bodily Care:			
1 Cor. 6:19,20	This represents good stewardship of my body.	_____	_____
Conscience:			
Romans 14:5	My sanctified conscience can be clear.	_____	_____

Therefore, at least at this stage, this activity is: _____ right
wrong _____ for me.

3. Is it right or wrong for me to try marijuana (or another drug, like cocaine) just once to see what it's like?
   (Be sure to do some fact-finding on this.)

Reference	Principle	True	False
Weight:			
Hebrews 12:1	It doesn't slow me down spiritually.	_____	_____
Profitability:			
1 Cor. 6:12a	It can be profitable, useful.	_____	_____
Control:			
1 Cor. 6:12b	I can be Spirit-controlled in this.	_____	_____
Bodily Care:			
1 Cor. 6:19,20	This represents good stewardship of my body.	_____	_____
Conscience:			
Romans 14:5	My sanctified conscience can be clear.	_____	_____

Therefore, at least at this stage, this activity is: _____ right
wrong _____ for me.

4. Is masturbating right or wrong for me?

Reference	Principle	True	False
Weight:			
Hebrews 12:1	It doesn't slow me down spiritually.	_____	_____
Profitability:			
1 Cor. 6:12a	It can be profitable, useful.	_____	_____
Control:			
1 Cor. 6:12b	I can be Spirit-controlled in this.	_____	_____
Bodily Care:			
1 Cor. 6:19,20	This represents good stewardship of my body.	_____	_____
Conscience:			
Romans 14:5	My sanctified conscience can be clear.	_____	_____

Therefore, at least at this stage, this activity is: _____ right
wrong _____ for me.

5. Try a question of your own.

Reference	Principle	True	False
Weight:			
Hebrews 12:1	It doesn't slow me down spiritually.	_____	_____
Profitability:			
1 Cor. 6:12a	It can be profitable, useful.	_____	_____
Control:			
1 Cor. 6:12b	I can be Spirit-controlled in this.	_____	_____
Bodily Care:			
1 Cor. 6:19,20	This represents good stewardship of my body.	_____	_____
Conscience:			
Romans 14:5	My sanctified conscience can be clear.	_____	_____

Therefore, at least at this stage, this activity is: _____ right
wrong _____ for me.

Well, how did you do? Needless to say, we have several qualifications to discuss; we'll get to those. But in the meantime, I hope you've caught the idea that exercising this Spirit-guided, Word-saturated method of finding out what's right and what isn't will force you further into the solid meat of God's thinking to "train your senses to discern good and evil" (Hebrews 5:14).

11
The Morals of the Story

Although self-righteousness is often viewed as a communicable disease, true righteousness before others will be viewed as an outright shock.

How do we do it? We're intimately tied to the God of truth; so how do we Christians so often make fools of ourselves, of Christianity, and ultimately of God Himself? One way we do it is by being judgmental. We don't need to shout or sling mud in order to reveal truth. Literally for Christ's sake, we must remember and respect each others' incredible value — unbelievers, too, have been made in the image of God (Genesis 1:27; James 3:9).

Within that respect for others, though, we must be solid on God's truth rather than on good human ideas or on the conventional wisdom of cultural Christianity.

Let's look at an example of a "truth" that gets a little muddy in its cultural-Christian version: the principle of not being a stumbling block. Paul writes in his letter to the Romans: "Determine . . . not to put an obstacle or a stumbling block in a brother's way" (Romans 14:13); "It is good not . . . to do anything by which your brother stumbles" (14:21). The King James Version translates verse 21 as "anything by which your brother is offended" — which muddies our understanding of what the stumbling block business is about. Christians sometimes presume that anything which offends the sensibilities of anyone is a stumbling block and is therefore wrong. A wonderful example of that conventional view is seen in Lady Gough's 1863 *Book of Etiquette* which mandated that the proper Christian bookcase provide separate shelves for books by single male authors and single female authors so as not to offend visitors. But let's look at the biblical concept of the stumbling block.

The words for "obstacle" *(proskomma)* and "stumbling block" *(skandalon)* don't mean actions that upset, offend or even irritate others. *Proskomma* is to cause another believer, by teaching or example, to violate his conscience. The primary New Testament example was the one just mentioned: Paul's discussion of encouraging weak, ex-idol-worshipping believers to eat meat offered to idols (Romans 14; 1 Corinthians 8; 10:23-31). *Skandalon* was originally the part of a trap to which the bait is attached, so the word signifies a snare or a trap.

Weak Christians have it tough enough with the stumbling blocks the world-system sets up (Matthew 13:41; 18:7). Why would a fellow believer add to the problem by kicking the weak brother when he's down, "wounding his conscience when it is weak" (1 Corinthians 8:12)? Setting up a stumbling block is serious sin (1 Corinthians 8:11-12) even though the activity involved can be perfectly harmless (Luke 17:1-2; Romans 14:16). The principle illustrates the fact that a good activity becomes evil (Romans 14:16) when it's not making us more Christlike. We can turn away from Him (1 Corinthians 8:12) by doing a "good" thing!

The stumbling block principle doesn't apply as you consider your actions in relation to other believers who are solid in their convictions; the principle is only violated in your relationship to weaker believers who will follow your lead — even to the point of violating their consciences.

Imagine the stumbling block principle in your mind's eye: See yourself running your race to become like Jesus Christ. You're running well. You see a fellow runner who's worn out; he's weak, not used to running. You decide to show off a little and jump a hurdle along the racetrack, and coax him to try jumping it as well. Or visualize yourself running a cross-country section of the racecourse, leading the weaker runner through a tricky, booby-trapped obstacle course. As a more experienced runner, you know where the traps are. He doesn't. And that's only the tip of the stumbling block iceberg; the Word has more to say on the subject.

But for now our discussion of the stumbling block principle illustrates a key point in knowing major-premise truths from the Word: Don't presume that conventional religious opinions parallel God's truth. Knowing major-premise truth isn't a cursory exercise of listening to people tell you about the Bible, reading someone's warm devotional thoughts in the mornings, or even scanning a chapter a day to keep the devil away. All these can channel you toward truth; but it's your personal, real involvement, understanding and adoption of the Word that gears you for discerning both good and evil. Remind yourself that you're not getting into the Word to find out information. You're getting into the Word to be changed. So don't fall for conventional Christian definitions, for generalized or second-hand thinking about God's values and ideas on topics from sex to evil to finances to violence. Be prepared to dump preconceived notions, to graciously rebel against old legalisms that announce, "Here is thy box, walk ye in it."

Don't fall for minor premises that are warped by prevalent legalistic ploys such as the following:

Guilt by association. Often, Christian speakers will warn us that certain literature, or music, or art, is evil because it's written, or performed, or executed by someone wicked. A kid's bizarre clothes aren't demonic just because they remind an elder of a newsphoto of the getups on a punk band that played a benefit for a political organization whose board has a member whose brother was a known homosexual who. . .

Faulty logic. A major premise of Scripture is that, since God lives in our bodies, we're separated to Him. Whole volumes on the "doctrine of separation" (see 2 Corinthians 6:14-18; Isaiah 52:11; Revelation 18:2-4) draw various lines. Some insist that Christians are wrong to look like non-Christians in dress style, make-up, hairstyle, formality or informality of appearance; wrong to act like non-Christians by joining certain organizations, enjoying some types of music; and wrong to be seen with non-Christians. It all depends on who's drawing the lines.

Of course, the world system referred to in Scripture is the Satan-controlled (1 John 5:19) organization of spirit henchmen (Ephesians 6:12) that influences humans through old nature desires (1 John 2:16). Of the seven possible meanings of the word *kosmos* (one of which is the world of people), this anti-God spiritual system is what we are to be separated from (see John 17:14-18).

Unfortunately, some have fallen into the faulty logic of this popular legalistic syllogism:
Major premise: Believers are to be separated from the world.

> Minor premise: The world is an anti-God spiritual system which can control non-Christians.
>
> Conclusion: Therefore it is wrong to look like, act like, or associate with non-Christians.

The syllogism operates on an emotional rather than logical level. Although the evil spiritual system of the world does influence non-Christians, it influences Christians as well — otherwise John wouldn't have warned us so severely about it (1 John 2:15,16). Although the world-system manifests its evil right and left in external things, concluding that the world-system is *inherent* in external things doesn't scripturally follow. Believers are to be separate from the sin of their surroundings. Our separating mark is this: Although we're in the thick of the world, we're not like the world in its lust of the flesh, lust of the eyes and boastful pride of life.

It's hard to understand why so many God-fearing, Bible-reading Christians determine their practical righteousness on a faulty-logic syllogism that says driving a new car is okay, but buying the latest fashion is not; wearing deodorant is wonderful, but wearing eyeshadow is demonic; using dramatic lighting on a nativity scene is stirring, but using dramatic lighting at a Christian concert is following the ways of the world. I think it has something to do with fear.

Ignorance. Ignorance is not stupidity. It's just not knowing the facts.

Books, by wild-eyed Christians, with never-before-revealed, startling conspiracies of evil often are documented with "proof" that turns out to be opinions and "facts" from conspiracy books by other wild-eyed authors. I once traced a decisive "proof" cited by a popular Christian author whose specialty is the evil of certain musical styles — only to find the "proof" text was quoted dishonestly out of context. We Christians are hard to take seriously sometimes, because we often get so easily zealous about a "righteous" position that hinges on a chock-full-of-baloney premise. U.S. Federal Communications Commission officials are undoubtedly still rolling their eyes at the literal roomsful of mail pouring in from Christians who oppose atheist Madalyn Murray O'Hair's proposal to ban religious broadcasting — even though O'Hair has never submitted any such proposal through the necessary legal channels, and even though the FCC has no intention of banning religious broadcasting. Yet the mail pours in, confirming that we're very concerned, but also very misinformed.

Am I being harsh on us? Sorry. My point isn't to hassle fellow believers who, because of upbringing or fear, are weak in honestly trusting what God has revealed rather than trusting what they think or feel. My point is to remind us that righteousness must be based on the razor-sharp truth of God's Word as major premises, on honest and well-informed truths about a situation as minor premises, and on truly Spirit-guided conclusions.

The Principle Of The Thing

Let's get into other major-premise truths.

Putting others before self. Do some serious renewed thinking through Romans 12:10,18; 1 Corinthians 10:23,24; Galatians 5:13; 6:5,10. Paul's key principle to the Philippians is worthy of hours of meditation:

> Do nothing from selfishness or empty conceit, but with humility of mind let each of you regard one another as more important than himself; do not merely look out for your own personal interests, but also for the interests of others. Have this attitude in yourselves which was also in Christ Jesus (Philippians 2:3-5).

For example, watch for the fine line between a legalistic view and a Spirit-guided view of the real-life norm of Christianity.

This isn't a "do-whatever-they-expect" principle; it's more a "dazzle-them-with-authentic-Christianity" — which might threaten their complacency. Incorporate our discussion on stumbling blocks into your very careful, mind-renewing thinking on Romans 14:13-23; 15:1-3; 1 Corinthians 8:1-13.

Edification. "All things are lawful for me, but not all things edify" (1 Corinthians 10:23). This principle involves a strong sense of actively building up your brothers and sisters in Christ. Edification can be accomplished through "varieties of gifts . . . and varieties of ministries . . . and varieties of effects" (1 Corinthians 12:4-6).

For instance, music can edify, not just through lyrics that "teach" listeners, but also by giving listeners opportunity to meditate on God or identify with an expression of spiritual sentiment. "Let us pursue the things which make for . . . the building up of one another" (Romans 14:19).

Evangelism. Here again, don't fall into the legalistic false logic that non-Christians will only be attracted to Christianity by people behaving in traditional religious ways. The circular conclusion of this false logic is that traditional appearances and activities are right and anything else is wrong. The focus of a Spirit-powered witness (Acts 1:8) is always in lifting up Jesus Christ (John 8:32), in making God "visible" (think through the paradox of God's invisible nature becoming visible — 1 John 4:7-12), by our agape (John 13:35) made practical in "good works" (Matthew 5:16). (See 1 Corinthians 9:19-22; 10:27-29; Colossians 4:5-6.)

Unequal ties. "Do not be bound together with unbelievers; for what partnership have righteousness and lawlessness, or what fellowship has light with darkness? Or what harmony has Christ with Belial; or what has a believer in common with an unbeliever? Or what agreement has the temple of God with idols? For we are the temple of the living God" (2 Corinthians 6:14-16).

"Bound" or "unequally yoked" is a word appearing only here in the New Testament, never in classical Greek texts nor the Septuagint. In context, the "unequal" is a fundamental difference in kind, in nature. The shades of fellowship that would violate this principle are delineated in five different words in the passage:

— "partnership" *(metoxe):* The verbal form of this word is translated "partner" in Luke 5:7, "partook" in Hebrews 2:14; and "belongs to" in Hebrews 7:13. "Having part with" is an English equivalent.

— "fellowship" *(koinonia):* Check back in Luke 5 to notice that the "partners" of verse 7 have a different relationship than do the partners *(koinonoi)* of verse 10. *Koinonia* denotes a close association of having everything in common (see in 1 Corinthians 1:9; 10:16; 2 Corinthians 13:14).

— "harmony" *(sumphonesis):* From sun — "with" — and phone — "voice" — , harmony is seen in our English transliteration "symphony." (See its use in Matthew 18:19 as "agree" and in Luke 5:36 as "match.")

— "in common" *(meris):* Meris denotes part of a whole, and so involves lot or destiny — "What destiny or part has a believer with an unbeliever?" (See John 13:8; Revelation 20:6; 21:8.)

— "agreement" *(sunkathathesis):* This word suggests a putting down or depositing along with someone. (See in Luke 23:50-51 where the verbal form is trans-"consented.")

If you will actually study through these passages and let your mind dwell on the words, you'll be heading toward God's ideas on the types of "yokes" to avoid.

Subjection to authorities. Remembering that they're only monitoring your life as allowed by your sovereign Authority, study Acts 4:18-20; Romans 13:1-7; Titus 3:1; 1 Peter 2:13-14; Ephesians 6:1-2; Hebrews 13:17. Notice that, while living in the context of an authority, a believer can ignore that authority's directives only when they violate explicit biblical commands or principles.

Subjection to parental authority is sometimes a sticky area of personal ethics. Parents (literally "ones who bring into becoming") are to be obeyed by children not because adults are always right, but for the child's training in obedience. How long should Junior obey his parents? As long as they are his literal "parents," the ones bringing him into who he'll be. Once parents have brought a child as far as they can into adulthood, another context supercedes and the son or daughter is commanded to honor that mother and father (Ephesians 6:1-2).

What about institutional authority such as Christian schools or missionary agencies? Does a Christian institution have a biblical right to compel conformity to its declared convictions? Briefly, consider the fact that the only biblical institution is the Church. And it's obvious in all that we're discussing that the Church is made up of believers who can justifiably have differing convictions — both in the universal Church of all believers and in a local church such as the one in Rome (Romans 14-15).

The norms that any Christian institution must maintain are the commands and principles of the Word. Beyond those, applications of scriptural principles are, according to New Testament doctrine, left to the individual believer. C. I. Scofield put it this way: "A church has no authority to decide questions of personal liberty in things not expressly forbidden in Scripture."

On the other hand, if a Christian school, mission agency, ministry or local church states that only believers who agree on particular convictions should join their ranks, it's certainly a believer's prerogative to decide to submit to restrictions based on those convictions if he wishes to join. For instance, it was worth it to me to enroll in a Christian school that offered some good teaching, even though I had to sign a statement that I'd not attend any movies; I voluntarily, freely gave up movie-going.

If the believer does not agree to abide by the convictions, he is not forced to join. If he does join, however, he must realize that those convictions aren't necessarily dictums to all Christendom. The basic question here, when being subject to an authority is optional, is: What authority should a Christian place himself under?

Exam Time

Get yourself situated in the Spirit, pray for wisdom, pick a right/wrong question and carefully deliberate whether God is telling you it's right or wrong in your life. Remember this is still only a glimpse of your developing ethical system since so few principles are represented. And remember too that if even one principle is violated, it's wrong for you. If a principle doesn't apply to your dilemma, simply leave that response blank.

For Study, Thought and Discussion

Run some of the following questions through the checklist below — even if you figure you've already arrived at a conclusion; and then run a few of your own right/wrong dilemmas through.

1. Is it right or wrong for me to dance? Is it right or wrong for me to go dancing at a place where alcohol is served?
2. Is it right or wrong for me to drive 57 m.p.h. if the limit is 55 m.p.h.?
3. Is it right or wrong for me to play cards?
4. Is it right or wrong for me to use profanity (words and phrases other than taking the Lord's name in vain) when I'm alone? When with close friends?
5. Is the way I make a living right or wrong as it affects others?
6. Are my bill-paying habits right or wrong?
7. How far (pick a specific point) can my physical contact with a member of the opposite sex go (pick a person) and still be right?
8. Is it right or wrong for me to join _____ (pick a particular club, organization or party)?
9. Is it right or wrong to marry a person of another race?
10. Is it right or wrong to report a friend who stole from his employer?

Reference	Principle	True	False
Weight:			
Heb. 12:1	It doesn't slow me down spiritually.	____	____
Profitability:			
1 Cor. 6:12a	It can be profitable, useful.	____	____
Control:			
1 Cor. 6:12b	I can be Spirit-controlled in this.	____	____
Bodily Care:			
1 Cor. 6:19,20	This represents good stewardship of my body.	____	____
Conscience:			
Rom. 14:5	My sanctified conscience can be clear.	____	____
Preference:			
Phil. 2:2	I can esteem others in this.	____	____
Example:			
1 Tim. 4:12	I can exemplify true Christianity.	____	____
Stumbling block:			
Rom. 14:13	This won't force a weaker brother to violate his conscience.	____	____
Edification:			
1 Cor. 10:23	This builds up fellow believers.	____	____
Evangelism:			
Col. 4:5	This demonstrates true Christianity to non-Christians.	____	____
Unequal yoke:			
2 Cor. 6:14	This won't intimately bind me to the old-nature pursuits of unbelievers.	____	____
Subjection:			
Romans 13:1	I can do this in submission to God's authorities over me.	____	____

Therefore, at least at this stage, this activity is: _____ right wrong _____ for me.

12
Only
The Beginning

Developing a system of personal rights and wrongs is just the beginning. We've been talking about scriptural principles in terms of our relationship with God and how they are expressed by the way we live out our ethical system. However, several foundational principles of Scripture focus simply on our relationship with God Himself. Two of these principles are stewardship and exaltation.

Stewardship

Everything belongs to God. "All things came into being by Him, and apart from Him nothing came into being that has come into being" (John 1:3). Take a good look around you right now; God either directly created what you now see, or the man-made things had their original source in Him. For instance, if you make money, it's because God allows you to: "Remember the Lord your God, for it is He who is giving you power to make wealth" (Deuteronomy 8:18). A basic tenet of discipleship is our renunciation of personal ownership over anything (see Luke 14:33).

One of the serious indictments against the nation of Israel was their tendency to forget God as the source of their material possessions; a tendency that repeatedly led to idolatry: "For [Israel] does not know that it was I who gave her the grain, the new wine, and the oil, and lavished on her silver and gold, which they used for Baal" (Hosea 2:8). Imagine borrowing $100 from the true love of your life, then using that $100 to pay for the sexual services of a prostitute or a gigolo. That's the force of a person's actions when he uses God's things for idol worship — whether the idol is the old self, or Satan. "You shall have no other gods before (or *besides)* Me" (Exodus 20:3) is reaffirmed in the New Covenant context in passages such as 1 Corinthians 8:4-6.

Mankind was originally given responsibility to care for God's creation (Genesis 1:25), and that mandate still carries into every area of our lives (see Luke 12:42-44). For instance, think carefully through more implications of treating your body as God's creation (1 Corinthians 6:18-20). We're even commanded to be good stewards of the abstracts of God's universe, as "stewards of the mysteries of God" (1 Corinthians 4:1).

Are "your" possessions windows to see Him, His provision, His goodness? Are they His to direct you to use or share? Or are they mirrors that flatly reflect you — your accomplishments, "your" ability to make wealth, your desires? Think of a possession. Is it only an enjoyment to you? Enjoyment is perfectly fine (1 Timothy 4:4). But enjoyment alone naturally breeds insecurity — ("What if I lose this and its enjoyment!") — and worry. Or is that possession an enjoyment and an *investment* (Matthew 6:9-21, 24-34; Luke 16:9-13; 1 Timothy 6:17-19)?

The stewardship principle is simple: God owns you and all your possessions; use them accordingly.

Exaltation

The exaltation principle is concerned with maintaining godly character, not before fellow believers, or before non-Christians, but before God. It might seem a little strange to live a godly life-style for God's benefit, as if we can impress Him. But it should be obvious by now in our studies that God wants to see God in us! Think through "glorifying" God as manifesting the reflection of what God is like.(See passages such as Romans 15:5-9; 1 Corinthians 6:20; 10:31.) Nothing should mar God's reflection in us; nothing should prevent the development of His qualities in us.

A related principle is seen in the New Testament injunctions to imitate God as He is revealed in Christ (see Ephesians 5:1-2). "The one who says he abides in Him ought himself to walk in the same manner as He walked" (1 John 2:6), tells us to emulate Christ's manner of life. The apostles never mentioned His appearance, so don't worry about having to wear sandals and flowing robes. The New Testament focuses on Christ's demeanor — on His simple but never petty conversations, on His compassion for the poor and sick, on His fierce fight against religious hypocrisy, on His strength in suffering, "leaving an example for you to follow in His steps" (1 Peter 2:21).

Let me offer a gentle warning here: Don't play with cartooned versions of this principle. In his 19th Century novel, *In His Steps,* Robert Shelton used as his measuring stick for righteousness the question, "What would Jesus do?" Since then, too many Christians have used that guide alone as their principle question for solving gray-area dilemmas. But if a person's old-nature-programmed image of Jesus is a meek and mild, Mona-

Lisa-faced cartoon, the principle is virtually worthless. That cartoon-Jesus can't be imagined playing linebacker for the Tennessee volunteers, or sunbathing on Santa Monica Beach, or selling deodorized shoe pads for a living in Casper, Wyoming, or marrying a woman named Zelda and having six screaming kids with braces and ingrown toenails. People who "do" those things can have the true nature of Jesus. Most people couldn't visualize a "Jesus" in those roles; but does that mean they're wrong? "Would Jesus be seen doing that?" is often unfairly used as a guilt tactic by adults who want to modify kids' behavior.

So be sure your emulation of God's character is based on the true character of God, of Christ — not merely on conventional ideas of who He is. Be like the God of the Bible. Pray, mull, and work through a Spirit-guided session to determine your personal ethics in areas like the following:

Are my personal budget appropriations right or wrong?

Is my reputation among _____ (pick a group of acquaintances) right or wrong?

Obviously, there are plenty of other principles to consider in a thorough determination of your personal ethics. For instance, consider whether a motive, attitude or action violates principles of:
— *honesty* (Proverbs 11:1; 2 Corinthians 8:21); I can be fair and honest with others in this.
— *forgiveness* (Leviticus 19:18; Matthew 18:21-22); What I'm doing has nothing to do with revenge.
— *world-system* conformity (Romans 12:2; 1 John 2:16); I'm not doing this just to go along with people who are controlled by the lust of the flesh, the lust of the eyes or the pride of life — whether non-Christian or Christian.
— *goodness* (Galatians 6:10); I must remember that good sometimes involves even painful discipline of

myself or others, and not giving in to others' destructive desires or behavior.

Run several of your own right/wrong questions through the checklist we've used earlier. Brace yourself; just one violation indicates that this isn't in God's plan for your best possible life, that it's wrong for you.

Questions

If you're fairly normal, undoubtedly all sorts of questions have popped into your mind as you approach this systematized look at personal ethics. Actually, I'd be worried if you didn't have quite a few questions; if you swallow this checklist idea *too* easily, it may indicate that you're not thinking it through carefully enough. Let's look at a couple of your questions.

Why just principles? We seem to have jumped into using only general principles in our final discussion of right and wrong, and the reasons for it are simple. First, matching an ethical question against an array of explicit biblical commands is a basic factor in personal ethics, but to do it in book form would require a mile-long list. And since the commands are explicit, all of them don't need consideration for just one activity. For instance, homosexual acts are wrong (Leviticus 18:22; 20:13; Romans 1:26-27; 1 Corinthians 6:9); adultery is wrong (Exodus 20:14; Matthew 5:28; Luke 18:20); cheating the government on taxes or any other way is wrong (Matthew 22:21; Romans 13:5-7). Besides, a list of commands as well as principles would make it just that much harder to convince you that I'm not advocating legalism (even though I'm advocating acknowledgement of laws), since legalists are famous for their lists. Legalists compile lists of do's and don'ts, while our checklist is simply a list of principles, not conclusions.

Finally, we're concentrating on principles because their potential for infinite application is God-designed for the fuzzy gray-area questions of right and wrong. You'll notice that if the application of a principle is itself a little fuzzy, consideration of other principles will clarify your deliberations.

Am I going to be tied to a mechanistic checklist? No. As we've seen, "solid food is for the mature, who because of practice have their senses exercised to discern good and evil" (Hebrews 5:14). The checklist approach is only a temporary method of emphasizing what needs to go on in your mind. The principles of Scripture must be such solid, clear factors in your thinking — not just in your brain, but in your mind and heart — that eventually any ethical question is matched automatically against an appropriate truth. But don't dismiss the checklist ideas as too elementary just yet; our tendency is to run one or two serious questions through the checklist and then go right back to the old, be-nudged-by-the-Spirit method of determining right and wrong. Ignore the tendency.

Our spiritual forefathers fought their way through ethical dilemmas in the past and handed their conclusions about Christian propriety down through the generations. Unfortunately, we in the cutting-edge present know all about those historical conclusions, but very little about the process of reaching conclusions. We've missed the whole point of righteous Christian living — that it's the process of determining and living righteousness that grows us, not the mindless parroting of others' conclusions — historic as they might be.

For a moment, let's consider the question: Is it right to legislate the personal morals of others? Aristotle was an early advocate of setting moral rules for those who, in his estimation, weren't rational enough to know what is good for them. These, Aristotle held, included children, women, and those who "by nature should be slaves"!

There's not much room for debate that an authority must legislate against individuals' actions that adversely affect others (Romans 13:1-4; 1 Peter 2:13-14), or that legislation must protect the moral development of children. But is it right to try to enforce my Christian convictions on other adults? What if their actions don't directly or indirectly affect the welfare of others? What if they affect only those who consent to be involved in the activity?

As creatures in the image of God, people have rights that are to be respected (Genesis 1:27; James 3:9).Think through the fine lines of legislating others' morals — from the Puritans' laws of mandatory Sunday worship, to ticketing those not wearing their seatbelts, to picketing adult X-rated theaters, to censorship of library books, etc.

Now, prayerfully depending on the Spirit for wisdom, answer this question: Is is right or wrong to legislate the personal morals of other people? Take the time to write out your answer, drawing your own line, and qualifying your statement as you feel appropriate.

Is your approach glorified situation ethics? Or is it biblical? We must be aware that biblical ethics recognizes the need of applying God's norms to real, specific situations, and it is possible for different believers to discover differing conclusions as the norms are applied — an activity can be right for one person in a particular setting and wrong for another.

Here are some nutshell differences between biblical ethics and situation ethics:

	Situation Ethics	Biblical Ethics
The Standards:	Love is only norm.	God's teachings, commands and principles are all norms.
The Reference:	An individual's idea of love.	God's authoritative Word.
The Deliberation:	An individual's old-nature-tainted reasoning and human wisdom.	New-nature absorption of the Spirit's guidance into truth and His wisdom.

What we've outlined is basically the difference between a good human-level set of ethics and divine
ethics. There are parallels; but only one system works.

Choices

Why do we often choose to do what's wrong? I'll
answer that from vast personal experience: Often I
choose wrong over right because of my lack of faith.
I think I know life better than God does. Remember
that faith isn't teeth-gritting auto-suggestion; it's deciding to trust, to adopt what God says.

Youth is a renowned era for lack of faith. That's
when it's easy to fall into a scientific-method version
of Christian ethics. Lack of experience is the young
person's excuse for experimentation. The rationale is,
How can you know a sexual affair is actually wrong
without experiencing it? (Of course, the same line of
reasoning can be extended to experimentation in snort-
ing cocaine, slitting a derelict's throat, or robbing a
church.) The idea is, "I don't agree with God's designa-
tion of wrong in this. Of course, I've never really
bothered to dwell on His truths about it — but life's
a rush. So maybe it's just bad for other people. It'll
be all right for me, because I'm not cut from the usual
mold. So I use the scientific method: I go ahead and

try it, repeat the experiment until I'm finally convinced it's wrong." We all do it in some way; we're sometimes determined to learn God's rights and wrongs the *hard way.*

Lack of faith is the meat of "Nobody knows, God can forgive me, so one little wrong won't hurt me," or "I don't care what God says about being able to escape temptations in 1 Corinthians 10:13, it's just not true for me."

Besides lack of faith, temptation is another reason we often choose what's wrong. Let's study through the essentials of temptation in James 1:13-15.

Satan's world system dangles an enticement or bait before one of your strong desires (usually a sin-nature-warped surface desire as described in 1 John 2:16: "For all that is in the world, the lust of the flesh and the lust of the eyes and the boastful pride of life, is not from the Father, but is from the world.") Your will then yields to the strong desire to embrace the enticement, and sin is born. Notice the desires of the body, soul and spirit involved in Eve's and Jesus' temptations (Genesis 3:1-6; Matthew 4:1-11).

Plot your own strategies for handling the temptations God allows in your life. The basic strategy, of course, is to know and trust the Word; your shield of faith quenches the fire in any temptation flung at you (Ephesians 6:16). That Word delineates three areas of temptation and three methods of handling them. When tempted physically, get literally or figuratively out of the situation (See Genesis 39:7-12; 2 Timothy 2:22). When tempted in the area of your soul — tempted by the "lust of the eyes" to look good, or have what you see — renew your commitment to serve and love God rather than to serve and love the world system (1 John 2:15) as Paul and John did (Acts 4:13-20). In that vague area of your spirit, temptations to dethrone God and be your own god are satanic attacks that are to be met by verbal resistance (James 4:7; Jude 9).

As you gain sensitivity to righteousness, expect tougher and more refined temptations to do wrong. An aged saint wouldn't have trouble countering "Hey, how about shooting up some smack tonight?" but might have a real struggle with a temptation to be envious.

Get Serious

Does this system of determining rights and wrongs focus too much on personal trivialities? Not at all.

In the first place, apparently insignificant rights and wrongs can be significant. In 1915 Leon Trotsky attended a Chicago Sunday School class in his search for truth. The teacher apparently thought that not notifying his class of his planned absence had nothing to do with ethics. The young men tried to hold their own session, but Trotsky, disgusted, left — and a few years later began turning whole countries upside down with socialist revolution. Mahatma Gandhi once closely studied Christianity but eventually rejected it because Christians didn't seem to live up to Christ's teaching. A frustrated Dallas youth worker thought he was right in telling a troublemaker never to come back to his church. Fifteen years later that troublemaker assassinated President John Kennedy. You know this: "insignificant" personal decisions do add up in the cause of righteousness.

In the second place, practicing biblical ethics in the less-than-monumental dilemmas of your personal life trains you to "discern good and evil" (Hebrews 5:14) in the complexities of ethics in the public sphere.

Is it spiritual to get involved in public ethics? The orator who said, "Let the clergy look after the things of the other world — I'll look after the things of this one," was Adolph Hitler. Too often Christians are scolded for getting involved in politics or social activism, and then political and social activist groups are scolded for being so godless. Biblical righteousness is designed to pervade politics, the fine arts, literature, labor unions, sports, social concerns, music, science, business, and cooking classes the way lights shine in the dark or the way salt flavors and preserves food (Matthew 5:13-16).

So first settle your own God-revealed personal ethics; then you can move into the more complex questions of our age. You'll find righteousness has a way of demanding responsibility in other areas.

Medical ethics. The midnight phone call shocked me: My brother had had a massive brain hemorrhage and was alive only because the hospital intensive care unit had hooked him up to a life support system. Even if he were to survive, the extensive brain damage meant he'd never come out of the coma. My dad drove me to the airport at 3:30 A.M. and said, "If it gets to a decision of pulling the plug or not, you are free to make the decision."

But as I slouched through the four-hour flight, I found I needed to pull out my own personal ethics, to finger the textures and truths of the principles and commands that apply to the taking of another's life. I had to look hard at the question of sustaining physical life when restoration to normal life is impossible, and at euthanasia.

With all the advances of medical science, and more on the horizon, plan on it: you'll sometime face or have to advise someone who's facing a dilemma like that of Mr. McKuen in the opening chapter sketch. Will you decide that letting a defective newborn die is right or wrong? Or how about deciding to switch off or leave on the life-support system of a loved one who'd die without it? Should the aged be allowed to die when they request that treatment be withheld? Are test-tube babies, surrogate mothers, or genetic engineering right or wrong?

Two good books to help you apply your personal ethics to these medical-ethics questions are Harmon L. Smith's *Ethics and the New Medicine* (Ann Arbor: Books on Demand, University Microfilms International) and James Hefley's *Life in the Balance* (Wheaton: Victor Books, 1980).

Incidentally, I never had to make that decision on my brother's life; he died eight minutes before I arrived at the hospital.

Socio-political ethics. Politics is a prime arena for the salt and light of personal Christian ethics to demonstrate true righteousness. Determine your own biblically-based positions on topics of economic ethics, on capital punishment and legal justice. Then you can confidently share the rationale of your convictions rather than fall back on cop-outs like "Well, my denomination says. . .," or "My pastor says. . .," or "My parents always used to say. . . ."

A dramatic example of the need for believers to announce their solid convictions in politics is seen in the nuclear weapons issue, which is essentially political. Determining your personal, Spirit-guided position is obviously critical to influencing others with your perspective on nuclear armament. Study reports, opinions, logistics, fact sheets and strategy briefs. Authoritative, concise information is easily available for both sides of the nuclear armament issue as well as from your local public library. Do some renewed thinking on your responsibility to pray for leaders, to be a peacemaker, to recognize government's role as God's agent for the punishment of lawbreakers with proportionate justice, to not shed innocent blood. (Sort carefully through Genesis 9:6; Exodus 20:13; 21:12-13; Joshua 8:1-29;

Judges 15:9-15; Psalm 94:20-21; 106:38; Proverbs 6:16-17; Jeremiah 22:15-17; Joel 3:19; Romans 13:1-7; 1 Timothy 2:2.)

Maybe you've put it off for too long already. Go ahead and use your personal ethics foundations to determine your social ethics positions on blockbusters such as abortion. (Think through Exodus 4:11; 21:22-25; Job 31:15; Psalm 139:13-15; Ecclesiastes 11:5; Isaiah 44:24; Jeremiah 1:5; Luke 1:26-56; Romans 14:22-23.)

The point is that with our study on personal Christian ethics, we've only scratched the surface of what it means to live in righteousness. So don't stop here.

Yeats wrote about the "widening gyre" of exponential military buildup, family breakdown, global economic labyrinths, oppression and spiritual fragmentation, and lamented that "the best lack conviction." So break the mold. Know. Live, and without apology announce: "This is what God says is right in my life." Unless individual believers in tiny victories live out the righteousness of Jesus Christ, Yeats will be right in concluding that "the centre cannot hold." The psalmist writes, "If the foundations be destroyed, what can the righteous do?" (Psalm 11:3).

So commit yourself to it: "Share His holiness" (Hebrews 12:10). Then . . . "the work of righteousness will be peace, and the service of righteousness, quietness and confidence forever" (Isaiah 32:17).

For Study, Thought and Discussion

Carefully answer these questions regarding legislating others' morals:

1. Are God's norms for believers only or for everyone?

2. Are believers' applications of God's norms for everyone?

3. Using several, specific, human vices as examples, determine whether the following is a true or false generalization: "Personal vices lead to wrongs that *do* adversely affect others."

4. Is the purpose of law — societies' laws included — to enforce goodness and godliness or to punish wrong-doing?

5. If you can convince an authority to adopt your Christian conviction as law, or if you are the authority (such as a parent), is it then right to enforce that conviction on others? If the authority doesn't adopt your conviction as law, have you the right to try to enforce it?

AUTHOR'S NOTE

At least pop music ethics are consistent: Back in the paisley '60s the Monkees crooned, "Today there is no wrong or right, only shades of gray"; in the leather-strapped '80s Queen crooned, "No wrong, no right, I'm gonna tell you there's no black and no white — just one vision."

Unfortunately, Christian ethics haven't enjoyed such singular vision. And maybe it's because we keep knocking our heads against ethics as a philosophy, as "a reconciliatory hope binding obedience to freedom in a corporate worldview of purity" — typical phrasing of ethical scholarship which, although true, only boggles the Christian Everyman who simply wants to know, "God, is this right?"

So although *Fine Lines* in no way discounts the profound work done in ethical theory, it does bypass most of the scholarly literature on ethics in order to get practical as painlessly as possible — which means our study won't encompass everything you always wanted to know about ethics.

We'll focus on personal ethics; with that base, you yourself can build a solid structure of social-institutional ethics. And I don't offer any erudite conclusions of right/wrong for you. *Fine Lines* just outlines the tools you need to fashion your own conclusions.

So roll up your sleeves and be prepared to do some serious thinking about the biblical system of ethics which not only reveals what's right and wrong for you but which also enables you to do what's right. Get good at the ethics that knock the stuffing out of spineless pop-Christianity, that firmly indict the thin-lipped legalism of "traditional" self-righteousness.

Instead of getting conformed to each other, let's surprise the world and get consistent about real righteousness.

Bill Stearns

Notes

Chapter 1

1. Arnold Brown, "The Age of Osiris," *Futurist* (April 1980), p. 23.

Chapter 2

1. C.S. Lewis, *Christian Behaviour* (New York: The Macmillan Co., 1943), p. 8.
2. Chuck Colson, *Born Again* (Old Tappan, NJ: Revell/Spire Books, 1977), p. 104.

Chapter 4

1. Oliver Barclay, "The Nature of Christian Morality," *Law, Morality, and the Bible,* eds., Bruce Kaye and Gordon Wenham (Downers Grove, IL: InterVarsity Press, 1978), p. 142.
2. Yannis Ritsos, "The Meaning of Simplicity," *Ritsos in Parentheses,* trans. Edmund Keeley (Princeton, NJ: Princeton University Press, 1979), p. 3.

Chapter 5

1. Francis Schaeffer, *True Spirituality* (Wheaton: Tyndale, 1972), p. 5.

Chapter 7

1. Tom Robbins, *Even Cowgirls Get the Blues* (New York: Bantam Books, 1976), pp. 191-92.

2. Anscombe, G.E.M., *Intention* (Oxford: Blackwell Publishing, 1957), p. 6.
3. Daniel Dennett, *Elbow Room: The Varieties of Free Will Worth Wanting* (Cambridge, MA: The MIT Press, 1984), pp. 169-70.
4. Liv Ullman, *Choices* (Toronto: Bantam Books, 1984), quoted from jacket back.

Chapter 9

1. James Packer, "Conscience, Choice and Character," *Law, Morality and the Bible,* eds., Bruce Kaye and Gordon Wenham (Downers Grove, IL: InterVarsity Press, 1978), p. 178.
2. Ruth Beechick, "Kholberg's Model of Moral Development," *Christianity Today* (December 30, 1977), p. 17.
3. C.S. Lewis, *Christian Behavior* (New York: Macmillan Co., 1946), p. 23.

Chapter 10

1. Twila Paris and Starla Paris, "Runner," © 1985 by StraightWay Music. Used by permission of Gaither copyright management.